In Pursuit of
PRIVACY

IN PURSUIT OF
PRIVACY

Law, Ethics, and the Rise of Technology

Judith Wagner DeCew

CORNELL UNIVERSITY PRESS
Ithaca and London

Library of Congress Cataloging-in-Publication Data

DeCew, Judith Wagner.
    In pursuit of privacy : law, ethics, and the rise of technology /
by Judith Wagner DeCew.
        p.   cm.
    Includes bibliographical references and index.
    ISBN 0-8014-3380-0 (cloth : alk. paper). — ISBN 0-8014-8411-1
(paper : alk. paper)
    1. Privacy, Right of—United States.   I. Title.
KF1262.D43   1997
342.73'0858—dc21   97-5409

Copyright © 1997 by Cornell University

First published 1997 by Cornell University Press.
First printing, Cornell Paperbacks, 1997.

Printed in the United States of America

Cornell University Press strives to utilize environmentally resposible suppliers
and materials to the fullest extent possible in the publishing of its books. Such
materials include vegetable-based, low-VOC inks and acid-free papers that are
also either recycled, totally chlorine-free, or partly composed of nonwood fibers.

Cloth printing   10 9 8 7 6 5 4 3 2 1
Paperback printing   10 9 8 7 6 5 4 3 2 1

In memory of my parents,
Sally Marsh Wagner
and
Robert Wanner Wagner

Contents

Acknowledgments

I began research on privacy when I studied as a Liberal Arts Fellow in Law and Philosophy at Harvard Law School during 1980–1981, on leave from the Department of Linguistics and Philosophy at the Massachusetts Institute of Technology. Subsequent work was supported in part by a 1984–1985 fellowship from the American Council of Learned Societies under a grant from the National Endowment for the Humanities and research time as a Fellow at the Bunting Institute at Radcliffe College during the fall of 1988. I am very appreciative of that support. I am also grateful to Clark University for the Alice Coonley Higgins Faculty Fellowship in Humanities for 1989–1990, as well as additional funding from the Higgins School of Humanities during 1990–1991 and from the Clark Faculty Development Fund during 1987–1988, 1989–1990, and 1990–1991. These grants provided me with access to the legal database Lexis, a part-time research assistant, and travel funding to present my material at professional meetings as well as at other colleges and universities.

This book was completed during 1993–1995 with the support of an NEH Research Grant for College Teachers and Independent Scholars, the Oliver and Dorothy Hayden Junior Faculty Fellowship from Clark University, and sabbatical leave from Clark University for the calendar year 1994. I am deeply thankful for the time and financial support that made completion of the project possible.

Part of an early version of chapter 2 was presented to the North American Society for Social Philosophy at the Western Division American Philosophical Association Meetings, May 2, 1986. Portions were also included in "The Poverty of Informational Privacy," delivered at the December 1985 Eastern Division APA meetings. William Parent was commentator, and I discuss his replies from those comments. A paper including parts of chapters 2 and 3 was presented at the University of Massachusetts at Amherst, the School for Urban and Public Administration at Carnegie-Mellon University, Wellesley College, Tufts University, and the Bunting Institute. I thank members of those audiences for their comments. I am especially indebted to Jonathan Adler, Sissela Bok, Leslie Burkholder, Joan Callahan, Peggy Carter, Joshua Cohen, Catherine Elgin, Fred Feldman, Jean Hampton, Michael Jubien, Hilde Nelson, Jonathan Pressler, Elizabeth Prevett, Lewis Sargentich, Ferdinand Schoeman, Thomas Scanlon, Laurence Thomas, and Kenneth Winston for helpful discussion and criticisms of material in the first three chapters.

A portion of chapter 4 was presented at a meeting of the Society for Philosophy and Public Affairs in honor of Ferdinand D. Schoeman, at the Eastern Division American Philosophical Association Meetings, December 29, 1993. Many thanks to Joan Callahan and Sidney Gendin for organizing the session. Diana Meyers, Melinda Roberts, Patricia Ewick, and Joan Callahan were especially generous with their time in providing comments on drafts of chapter 5, and I am also grateful to Clark colleagues for their discussion at a colloquium where I presented my work on the feminist critique of privacy. An earlier version of chapter 7 was presented at Hampshire College. I am indebted to Ilona Bell, Marlene Fried, Jay Garfield, and Kenneth Winston for their useful suggestions.

I am grateful to Dr. Miriam Mazor and Hilde Nelson for valuable materials and comments regarding chapter 8. Portions of chapter 9 were delivered on November 11, 1993, at an international conference, "Philosophy and Information Technology," at Erasmus University in Rotterdam, the Netherlands, organized by Jeroen van den Hoven. My sincere thanks to him, to Julie Inness, and to other participants at that conference for helpful comments. Paul Burke, Kate Chesley, Alison Jennings, and Mary Mitchell also gave me information and suggestions on drafts of that paper, and I am especially indebted to Ross E. Mitchell for our collaboration on privacy issues surrounding caller identification.

Several editors have kindly permitted me to use parts of articles I originally published in their journals. Material in chapters 2 and 3 appeared in an early form in two of my essays: "The Scope of Privacy in Law and Ethics," *Law and Philosophy* 5, 2 (1986), 145–173, copyright © 1986 by Kluwer Academic Publishers, reprinted in *The Nature and Process of Law*, ed. Patricia Smith (Oxford: Oxford University Press, 1993), 715–726, and "Defending the 'Private' in Constitutional Privacy," *The Journal of Value Inquiry* 21 (1987), 171–184, copyright © 1987 by Kluwer Academic Publishers; both are used with kind permission of Kluwer Academic Publishers. A portion of chapter 5 appeared in an early form in the American Philosophical Association *Newsletter on Philosophy and Law and Feminist Philosophy* 94, 2, ed. Rex Martin and Hilde Hein (1995), 42–45. A section of chapter 6 and much of chapter 7 appeared in an early form in my article "Constitutional Privacy, Judicial Interpretation, and *Bowers v. Hardwick*," *Social Theory and Practice* 15, 3 (1989), 285–303, reprinted in part in "The Future of Privacy: Assessing the Supreme Court's Antisodomy Decision," *Radcliffe Quarterly* 25, 1 (1989), 14–18. Chapter 8 originally appeared as "Drug Testing: Balancing Privacy and Public Safety," *Hastings Center Report*, 24, 2 (1994), 17–23, reprinted in *Social Issues Resources Series: Privacy*, vol. 5, article 28 (1994), hardcopy and CD-ROM; reproduced by permission, © The Hastings Center. A short portion of chapter 9 appeared in an early form in Ross E. Mitchell and Judith Wagner DeCew, "Dynamic Negotiation in the Privacy Wars," *Technology Review* 97, 8 (1994), 70–71.

I want to express my appreciation to the graduate faculty of the philosophy department at the University of Massachusetts at Amherst and to John Ackerman, director of Cornell University Press, for steady support. I am particularly grateful to my editor, Alison Shonkwiler, for all her guidance and enthusiasm. My thanks go to Alice Falk for helpful copyediting. I am also grateful to Linda Jorge, my Clark student and research assistant, Sean Parker and Alexandra Polier, our work-study students, and Carmella

D'Ambra, our administrative secretary, for their tireless efforts. This book is dedicated to my parents, Sally and Bob Wagner, who always believed in my achievement and promise, who encouraged me to do the best possible and to be everything I could be, and who as models helped me learn how to balance career and parenting. They were always there to support me and my family, in tears or in laughter, and I thank them with all my heart.

None of this work would have been possible without the co-operation of David, Melissa, and Jeffrey, who learned to allow me to closet myself in my study, and without the cheerful and constant encouragement from my husband, Lanny. There are not sufficient words to thank you.

JUDITH WAGNER DeCEW

West Newton, Massachusetts

In Pursuit of
PRIVACY

Introduction

The concept of privacy is a central one in most discussions of modern Western life, yet only recently have there been serious efforts to analyze just what is meant by "privacy." Much of the current discussion of privacy evolved from a constellation of legal judgments. Philosophers then entered the debate, attempting to illuminate what a right to privacy can and should mean. In both law and ethics, "privacy" is an umbrella term for a wide variety of interests. We might agree that information such as the content of one's fantasies is private. And there is consensus that action such as wife battering, even if done in the confines of one's home, is not wholly private. Nevertheless, there are troubling borderline cases. For example, should threats on another's life, made in confidence to a lawyer or psychiatrist, be protected in the name of privacy?[1] It seems complexities concerning the relationship of privacy and harm (or risk of harm), and the conflict between privacy and social good, have yet to be sorted out to determine how important or abusive information or conduct must be before it is no longer private in these kinds of cases.

In chapter 1 I discuss origins of privacy as a concept, stressing its fundamental role in language and thought, in contexts both older and broader than contemporary discussions of privacy generally acknowledge. This discussion will help corroborate my appeals in subsequent chapters to the ordinary use of language, to the clusters of interests encompassed by privacy, and to intuitions about privacy's importance and scope. I also discuss the history of privacy protection in American law, describing the wide range of cases that have been thought to have privacy aspects. Owing to the growth of computer technology and capacities for electronic

1

surveillance and for data collection and storage, there has been increased concern about protection from unwarranted observations and exploitation of personal communications and information including academic, medical, and employment records. In these areas privacy is most obviously at stake, and it has traditionally been protected in tort law as an interest in "having control over information about oneself" and under the Fourth Amendment protection against search and seizure. In addition, privacy has been associated in constitutional law with matters such as possession of obscene material in one's home, interracial marriage, attendance at public schools, sterilization, contraception, abortion, and other medical treatment.

This two-pronged development of privacy protection in tort and constitutional law is peculiar and complex. Explication of the diversity of cases invoking privacy introduces a major cause of disagreement over how extensive privacy protection should be, as well as emphasizing the many areas of our lives affected by alternative views on privacy. Although this material on legal history is familiar to some, it makes the subsequent arguments accessible to those who may have little knowledge of the many privacy cases.

Chapter 2 focuses on the *legal* line of argument concerning ambiguities surrounding the historical divergence between "tort" and "constitutional" privacy. Because there is no right to privacy explicitly guaranteed in the Constitution and because the right to privacy has been invoked in such diverse cases, the constitutional right to privacy has been severely criticized since the notion was first suggested.[2] William Parent, Louis Henkin, and others have held that the only legitimate use of the term "privacy" is to refer to informational privacy.[3] They argue, moreover, that the controversy surrounding constitutional privacy can be resolved if it is recognized that despite the Supreme Court's reliance on a right to privacy, the constitutional cases have "no basis in any meaningful conception of privacy" and are concerned solely with an interest in autonomy or liberty in some sense.[4]

I discuss two defenses of this narrow view of privacy. First, I examine and criticize William Parent's definition of privacy for the law, which leads to an examination of what sorts of privacy protection are omitted if only informational privacy is guaranteed. Second, I present and reject Henkin's formulation in terms of autonomy, together with Parent's alternative version in terms of liberty, of the argument that appeals to "privacy" in the constitutional cases conflate privacy with autonomy or liberty. My goals in this chapter are (i) to explain the narrow view of privacy, (ii) to indicate how pervasive this view is among legal theorists such as Henkin, Hyman Gross, and Richard Posner, as well as among philosophers such as Parent and Judith Thomson, and (iii) to criticize this narrow view. My critique demonstrates the implausibility of the narrow view and sets the stage for defending a broader conception.

In chapter 3 I turn to a second line of argument, which focuses on the most important *philosophical* responses to the confusion surrounding the meaning and scope of the concept of privacy. Judith Thomson has argued that there is no such thing as *the* right to privacy since any privacy right can be explained in terms of other rights, notably property rights and rights to bodily security.[5] But as Thomas Scanlon and others have persuasively countered, it is surely *as* plausible that just the reverse is true, that rights such as those of ownership or even liberty are "derivative" from privacy rights.[6] Scanlon apparently finds this ordering likely since he believes there is something unique and of special value in privacy. On that point I agree with him. I show, however, that attempts to give a unitary definition of privacy in terms of secrecy and concealment, seclusion, and confidential content neither match nor explain common moral intuitions on privacy. In addition, theories based on control, property, and intimacy[7] are inadequate to explain the depth and range of privacy claims.

I also explore and discuss conceptual alternatives that allow for a broad and inclusive account of privacy, addressing the difficulties of explaining the existence of justifiable invasions of privacy and of understanding how the protection of privacy preserves liberty. I then argue that a broad characterization of privacy that appeals to a "reasonable person" standard can be adapted to allow for reasonable but divergent perspectives on what is worthy of protection in the name of privacy.

One lesson from the first three chapters is that it is not possible to give a single, unitary definition that covers the many diverse privacy interests. Clearly there is some intuitive difference between tort and constitutional privacy, described by the Supreme Court as (i) an "individual interest in avoiding disclosure of personal matters" and (ii) an "interest in independence in making certain kinds of important decisions."[8] But that need not mean the wide range of privacy claims are unrelated. As Scanlon says, even if privacy violations are many and diverse, and do not derive from any single, overarching right, they may yet have a common foundation. I argue in chapter 4 that similarities exist among these varied privacy claims which are philosophically well motivated, historically accurate, and familiar in our common use of language, to show that even when autonomy is involved, the constitutional cases *do* raise genuine privacy concerns.

I present a strong positive argument for defending privacy as an inclusive concept by documenting the similarity of reasons cited in tort, Fourth Amendment, and other constitutional cases for protecting control over information as well as control over decision making—reasons such as freedom from scrutiny and judgment, and protection from pressure to conform. Recent reflections on privacy by Ferdinand Schoeman highlight important social dimensions of privacy that are often neglected, and I use these to supplement more traditional understandings of privacy claims. I then defend privacy as a broad and multifaceted cluster concept and mark out the contexts where it is natural to view privacy as crucial, by characterizing fundamental aspects of it that are familiar in our general usage of the term and that are at issue in tort, Fourth Amendment, and other constitutional cases. My approach to a full understanding of privacy has two main themes. First, I identify and describe three major clusters of interrelated claims, indicating how they are connected by the underlying values and reasons used to justify their protection. Second, I propose a strategy of beginning with a presumption in favor of protecting privacy in these contexts. While that presumption can be overridden or rebutted, it establishes the importance of privacy as a fundamental value that must then be balanced against other individual and social interests. In subsequent chapters I select particular cases to illustrate how that balancing can be accomplished so that privacy is respected even when it conflicts with other claims and values.

In chapter 5 I address a difficult challenge to privacy, namely whether and how we can recognize the "darker side of privacy" articulated by feminists while embracing the value of privacy for protecting a sphere within which we can fend off intrusion and scrutiny by others. According to the feminist critique, privacy can be used to shield domination, repression, degradation, and even physical harm to women and others. Granting special status to privacy protection is thus detrimental to women because the powerful use it to dominate and control women, to enforce the silence and helplessness of women, and to cover up abuse. Therefore privacy is seen as a tool to sustain and increase the marginalization of women and others without power.

In response to this critique, some feminists have suggested abandoning defenses of privacy protection. Other feminists including myself recognize and appreciate the feminist critique, yet have long defended the value of privacy protection and sought a way to reconcile these apparently conflicting views. I focus on one prominent version of this attack on privacy, articulated by Catharine MacKinnon and others.[9] I describe and analyze alternative interpretations of MacKinnon's rejection of the public/private distinction, arguing that though we may endorse major portions of the feminist critique of privacy, nevertheless, on either interpretation of the feminist critique, a meaningful concept of privacy can be retained and defended.

Chapters 6 and 7 address applications of my theory to questions about sexual and reproductive privacy raised in landmark cases of the past twenty-five years, to illuminate our understanding of those cases. Chapter 6 explores an important implication of my view that privacy has broad scope: that it extends to the constitutional cases, including the famous and controversial 1973 abortion decision *Roe v. Wade*. In particular, I show that criticism of *Roe v. Wade* does not undermine my defense of privacy. After explaining alternative views of judicial interpretation, in part to defeat the claim that we must reject constitutional privacy on the grounds that it is not explicitly written into the Constitution, I utilize the discussion of theories of adjudication to assess the extent to which embracing a broad notion of privacy is compatible with John Hart Ely's devastating critique of *Roe v. Wade*.[10] Ely's critique grows out of his views on constitutional interpretation and judicial protection of minorities as defended in *Democracy and Distrust*.[11] I show how Ely's criticism can be explained in terms of disagreement over the stringency of fetuses' and mothers' rights or claims, without denying that an important privacy interest is relevant. This adds support to my thesis that the presence of an autonomy interest does not undercut the view that the constitutional cases involve a meaningful and important notion of privacy.

Chapter 7 addresses another major implication of my interpretation of privacy, namely the extent to which a broad view allows justification of the legislation of morals in either sexual or nonsexual contexts. Careful reexamination of arguments concerning privacy and the enforcement of morals is particularly important given their prominence in the Supreme Court's 1986 privacy decision, *Bowers v. Hardwick*, upholding Georgia's anti-sodomy laws.[12] Chief Justice Burger's concurring opinion concluded in particular, "To hold that the act of homosexual sodomy is somehow protected as a fundamental right would be to cast aside millennia of moral teaching." I criticize White's view and assess other arguments in the *Bowers* case, relating them to arguments by H. L. A. Hart and Patrick Devlin in their famous debate on decriminalization of homosexuality and prostitution.[13] That debate substantiates the claim that privacy is relevant in the *Bowers* case and generates further conclusions on the enforcement of morals and the future of privacy.

I focus in chapters 8 and 9 on privacy issues raised by public safety concerns and developing technology that are not limited to sexual and reproductive privacy. Chapter 8 addresses the tension between privacy and drug testing programs aimed at enhancing public safety. This conflict is provocative because it highlights the links between privacy interests previously treated separately in tort and constitutional law. I explain arguments both for and against drug-testing programs, including issues about the accuracy of tests and the handling and interpretation of results, and I describe the constitutional guidelines developed for such programs thus far. After detailing the full range of privacy concerns compromised by drug testing, from control over information and Fourth Amendment search and seizure to control over one's body, I explain narrow conditions under which drug-testing programs can be morally justified. It is possible to address major health and safety goals adequately while also taking precautions to protect privacy vigorously.

I turn in chapter 9 to ways in which technological advance increases threats to privacy, particularly with database information storage and new telephone and computer services such as caller identification and e-mail. For both types of cases there are ways of allowing the new technologies to flourish while managing them appropriately to protect privacy through the development of reasonable federal regulations. It is possible to ensure that individuals are able to choose whether and when to forfeit their privacy without losing the benefits of these new technologies. These contemporary cases demonstrate the importance and advantages of beginning with presumptions in favor of privacy protection, and then developing ways to allow individuals to determine for themselves how and when that presumption should be overridden.

Supreme Court confirmation hearings over the past few years have emphasized the importance of my central goal: providing a firmer philosophical foundation for future discussions of privacy doctrines in tort and constitutional law. Reaction to Judge Bork's nomination and the subsequent congressional hearings before the appointments of Justices Kennedy, Souter, Thomas, Ginsberg, and Breyer have made it clear that many in the public and in Congress are unwilling to give up the protection of privacy they currently enjoy. Since current constitutional standards require "strict scrutiny" for cases concerning "fundamental values," and privacy has been judged to be one such value, we must establish whether or not the ancillary issues—obscenity in one's home, sterilization, contraception, abortion, consenting homosexuality, drug testing, and so on—involve a significant interest in privacy, not merely autonomy. If so, those privacy claims have a *better* chance of being protected than they would have if only freedom from governmental interference were involved. In sum, it has been my aim to articulate and unify diverse strands of argument in legal and philosophical inquiries as they relate to the extent privacy protection is and should be guaranteed in a wide variety of contexts in contemporary life.

Origins and History
of Privacy

In the United States, formal legal protection for privacy has developed only during the last hundred years. Nevertheless, the concept of privacy has older and far deeper roots than contemporary legal and philosophical discussions normally acknowledge.[1] Some concept (or multiple concepts) of privacy has played a fundamental role in political and religious writings as well as in biological, anthropological, and sociological studies from antiquity to today. There is ample evidence for this, some of which is explicit in or can be inferred from written material, and some of which derives from customs and social practices. Together, these sources demonstrate that the theoretical and conceptual foundations of some notion of privacy are well established.

Consider first some examples of written references to a concept of privacy. Within political theory, an important and well-known (though sometimes controversial) tenet since the time of Aristotle has been the dichotomy between public and private realms. Jean Bethke Elshtain has argued that a wide array of thinkers "of the Western political tradition assumed and deployed *some* form of a distinction between the public and the private as conceptual categories and as private and public imperatives, to conceal as well as reveal. As conceptual categories, public and private ordered and structured diverse activities, purposes, and dimensions of human social life and thinking about that life.''[2] The public/private distinction has sometimes been taken to reflect differences between the appropriate scope of government, as opposed to self-regulation by individuals. It has also been interpreted to differentiate political and domestic spheres of life. These diverse linguistic descriptions capture overlapping yet nonequivalent concepts. Nevertheless they share the assumption that there is a boundary marking off that which is private from that which is public.

Aristotle saw the polis, the concept of a structured body politic and province of political activity, as a public sphere where details of government and the proceedings of the city-state developed.[3] Political animals by nature, men (but not women or slaves or children) were intended to participate fully in the polis. In ancient times as well as later, the trend was to set limits on the power of governmental authority by separating from this public sphere various places and activities viewed as illegitimate arenas for public regulation. As Jürgen Habermas notes, "In the fully developed Greek city-state the sphere of the *polis*, which was common (*koinē*) to the free citizens, was strictly separated from the sphere of the *oikos*; in the sphere of the *oikos*, each individual is in his own realm (*idia*)."[4] For Aristotle the *oikos* was a private sphere attached to the home, namely the private household. Thus family life served as a paradigm of the private sphere that defined the role of women. A male citizen's status in the polis depended on his unlimited and dominant status as master in the *oikos*.[5] For subsequent authors, a broader array of activities beyond those of family, reproduction, birth, and death were included in the private sphere; other activities deemed individual or religious, for example, were not held open to public governance.

A second instance in political literature comes from John Locke, who marked off the distinction between public and private property explicitly in his *Second Treatise on Government* (1690). The original state of nature, according to Locke, is for all "a state of perfect freedom to order their actions, and dispose of their possessions and persons as they see fit, within the bounds of the Law of Nature.''[6] In the state of nature no person has exclusive rights to the earth. The earth and all the bounty produced by nature belong to all in common. Nevertheless, each person possesses himself (or herself) absolutely and has property rights to that with which he mixes his labor. Everyone has a property right to ''his own person'' and can extend it through sweat and labor. Thus what belongs to and is acquired by the self is private property and is distinctly separate from what is owned publicly or in common with all. In Locke's *Treatise* there are other contexts in which the separation between public and private remains, yet the relationship between the spheres is more complex. Those who freely consent to create a political society thereby establish public means, namely the maintenance of civic order through social contract, to assure private ends, specifically the protection of life, liberty, and property. In contrast to Aristotle's view, the state becomes for Locke a necessary means for public protection of certain private ends.[7]

As a third example, Milton Konvitz has called attention to ways in which biblical passages can be interpreted as distinguishing a realm of privacy:

Almost the first page of the Bible introduces us to the feeling of shame as a violation of privacy. After Adam and Eve had eaten the fruit of the tree of knowledge, ''the eyes of both were opened, and they knew that they were naked; and they sewed fig leaves together and made themselves aprons.'' Thus, mythically, we have been taught that our very knowledge of good and evil—our moral nature as men—is somehow, by divine ordinance, linked with a sense and a realm of privacy. When, after the flood, Noah became drunk, he ''lay uncovered in his tent,'' and Ham violated his father's privacy by looking on his father's nakedness and by telling his brothers about it. His brothers took a garment, ''laid it upon their shoulders, and walked backward and covered the nakedness of their father. Their faces were turned away, and they did not see their father's nakedness.''[8]

In addition to these historical references to a distinction between public and private, consider as well biological and anthropological studies that provide evidence of the fundamental value placed on privacy. Alan Westin has reviewed animal studies demonstrating that a desire for privacy is not distinctively human.[9] Such studies show, for example, that virtually all animals seek periods of individual seclusion or small-group intimacy. Usually described as a tendency toward territoriality, such patterns serve various biological purposes, especially that of ensuring propagation of the species. Westin concludes that "the parallels between territory rules in animal life and trespass concepts in human society are obvious: in each, the organism lays claim to private space to promote individual well-being and small-group intimacy."[10]

Elshtain has claimed that "distinctions between public and private have been and remain fundamental, not incidental or tangential, ordering principles in all known societies save, perhaps, the most simple."[11] She is quick to point out, moreover, that even in primitive societies activities are ordered and differentiated by taboo and shame: those that can be seen by others are distinguished from those that are carried out under cover. Anthropological studies by Margaret Mead and others, as well as social and psychological research, support this view that privacy is a cross-cultural and cross-species universal.[12] They have shown that virtually all societies have techniques for setting distances and avoiding contact with others in order to establish physical boundaries to maintain privacy. Concealment of the female genitals, seclusion at moments of birth and death, the preference for intimacy for sexual relations (usually performed away from the view of others or at least away from the view of children), restricted rules of entry into homes by nonresidents, and the secrecy of group ceremonies are the most common examples of setting such boundaries.

Although some primitive cultures appear to show no concern for privacy for changing clothes, bathing, birth, death, and even excretion, anthropologists have found that these cultures use various psychological methods for gaining privacy for the individual or family when communal life makes such physical privacy protection impossible. Thus, restriction of access to oneself or the flow of information about oneself by withholding feelings and expression, averting one's eyes, facing a wall, and so on provide more subtle ways of putting up social barriers.[13] The nearly universal need to protect a private sphere is further documented by the nearly universal tendency of societies to engage in surveillance to guard against intrusions on privacy by individuals, intrusions that violate the group norms.[14] Aggressive enforcement of social rules and taboos protecting privacy emphasizes the value placed on privacy protection.

The sources and literature I have briefly surveyed are quite varied. It is worth emphasizing that despite the importance placed on privacy in each one, the idea of privacy employed is not always the same. Privacy may refer to the separation of spheres of activity, limits on governmental authority, forbidden knowledge and experience, limited access, and ideas of group membership, to name a few possibilities. Consequently, this background sketch provides evidence that privacy is commonly taken to incorporate different clusters of interests.

Anthropological literature documents the increased physical and psychological opportunities in modern societies to gain privacy through anonymity, mobility, and economic autonomy. At the same time, however, greater population density, technological advances, and increased governmental power all undermine an individual's ability to maintain a private space within a broader social community.

It is likely that technological advance was a major impetus for the codification of privacy protection in written law in the United States. Privacy had for some time been guarded by individuals interacting and enforcing social customs. From the end of the nineteenth century on, however, the development of widespread communication through newsprint, the growth of mass transportation, and inventions such as the telephone and radio made informal methods of privacy protection both insufficient and ineffective. Development of the microphone and digital recorder, as well as the capacity to tap telephones, added to the technologies that made eavesdropping and electronic surveillance an increasing threat.

Two Interests in Privacy in the Law

American law has evolved to protect two apparently different rights to privacy—one developed in the last ninety years in tort and Fourth Amendment law, the other first announced as a constitutional right in 1965. Taken within the context of the large portion of U.S. law that derives from English common law, both are relatively recent developments.

Much of the vast literature on privacy has focused on the interest protected in tort law that is referred to as the crucial core of privacy; it is often described as "having control over information about oneself." Perhaps the earliest mention of privacy concerns appeared in 1880 in Judge Thomas Cooley's legal treatise on torts, where he included the "right to be let alone," which he called a right to one's person and a right of personal immunity.[15] Along with other suggestive language, the term "privacy" was then invoked explicitly a year later in *DeMay v. Roberts*, a case granting tort relief to a woman whom the defendant observed during childbirth without her consent. Although the charge in the case was battery, not invasion of privacy, the Michigan Supreme Court unanimously agreed that the "plaintiff had a legal right to the privacy of her apartment at such a time, and the law secures to her this right by requiring others to observe it, and to abstain from its violation."[16]

A far more detailed appeal for privacy protection appeared in one of the most influential law review articles ever written, "The Right to Privacy" by Samuel Warren and Louis Brandeis. Arguing that "political, social, and economic changes entail recognition of new rights" and "the common law . . . grows to meet the demands of society,"[17] Warren and Brandeis urged that protection against actual bodily injury (battery), attempts (assault), nuisances (offensive noises and odors), slander, and even alienation of a wife's affections (which was held remediable!)[18] be supplemented with a right to privacy protecting a person even if the injury is merely to individual feelings. Relying on Judge Cooley's phrase, the right "to be let alone," and cases they felt were already precedents, they argued that the law should "protect the privacy of private life"[19] by securing for an individual the right of determining the extent to which his or her written work, thoughts, sentiments, or likeness could be given to the public. Citing recent inventions and numerous mechanical devices such as high-speed cameras and presses for mass production of newspapers that "have invaded the sacred precincts of private and domestic life,"[20] they held that for years there had been a sense that the law needed to offer a remedy for protection from such invasions.

According to one story, recounted by Dean William Prosser,[21] a major motivation for the Warren and Brandeis article was Warren's distress about newspaper publicity concerning his daughter's wedding. That has been disputed. But if there was any reporting of family affairs that troubled Warren, it highlights the early link between technological advances, in this case the use of large-scale media coverage through newspapers, and growing worries about protecting individual privacy.

Up until 1890 the law had been extremely cautious about protecting emotional harms for at least two reasons: (i) the difficulty of assessing damages for emotional harms and (ii) the subjectivity of the findings based on a state of mind, especially where there is no parallel or concomitant physical injury. While the second is perhaps a reasonable concern, the first is a poor excuse for denying recovery. Surely it is no less difficult to fix a dollar value on a finger lost, an arm, or a life. But Warren and Brandeis were arguing that existing law already recognized a principle of privacy derived from common law in such cases as breach of trust and defamation, which, when applied to new facts, could protect individuals from the press, photographers, or anyone with devices for recording or reproducing sounds or scenes. Thus they claimed *not* to be advocating judicial legislation or the addition of legal principles by judges.[22]

Warren and Brandeis's description of their vision of the nature and extent of the privacy right provides insight into why protection of the right was viewed as important, and it even appears to anticipate some of the subsequent controversy surrounding privacy. In defending a general right to privacy for thoughts, emotions, and sensations in any form, Warren and Brandeis focused particularly on a privacy right that gives an individual the power to control absolutely the limits of publicity about him- or herself. As part of the general right of an individual to be let alone, which they also described as the general right to immunity of the person and the right to one's personality, they emphasized that privacy is not a property right. In personal letters, for example, it is not the intellectual product that is protected but the "domestic occurrence." The underlying principle invoked is the protection of an "inviolate personality."[23] The right, they believed, arises from the peace of mind or relief afforded by the ability to prevent publication.

To give a partial illustration of the protection they defended, Warren and Brandeis urged repression of publicity concerning the private life, habits, acts, and relations of individuals, where these have no connection to the individuals' fitness for public office. They pointed out, however, that the right to privacy was incapable of being given an exhaustive and wholly accurate definition; it would instead be worked out through opinions in a vast number of cases. That process would be possible, they felt, due to the law's elasticity, capacity for growth, and adaptability to new conditions in the face of modern devices affording more abundant opportunities for the perpetration of such wrongs as they had described.

Despite their emphasis on the excesses of the press, Warren and Brandeis stressed that privacy is essential to provide a sanctuary or retreat from the increasing complexity and intensity of life resulting from a wide array of technological advances. Thus the article suggests the authors felt more was at stake than anxiety, embarrassment, or hurt feelings caused by unwelcome publicity. Their discussion of "inviolate personality" indicates their concern for values that might today be described using terms such as "personhood" and "self-identity." Yet ironically, the defense of a legal interest often exposes one to further harms. Pursuing protection and damages in court for the right that Warren and Brandeis defended often requires exposure and more loss of the very same kind of privacy.

While the earliest test cases failed to protect the right Warren and Brandeis argued for,[24] both the public and subsequent cases soon endorsed and expanded it. The Georgia Supreme Court was the first to recognize and affirm a legal right to privacy in *Pavesich v. New England Life Insurance Company* in 1905.[25] Whereas Warren and Brandeis appealed in their essay to the recognition of privacy within common law, the *Pavesich* court offered several different kinds of argument in an attempt to establish a foundation for recognizing the new right. In particular, the court cited the right of privacy as having "its foundation in the instincts of nature" and as being "therefore derived from natural law." The right to withdraw from the public gaze was, the court argued, "embraced within the right of personal liberty." According to the unanimous ruling, the use of the plaintiff's photograph without his consent was unauthorized, unjustifiable, and an "invasion of the rights of his person." Thus in its early recognition, the privacy right protected in tort law was not referred to in terms of protection of information alone. To the contrary, it was broadly recognized as part of common law as well as the true principles of justice embodied in natural law, connected with concepts of liberty and personhood now familiar in constitutional cases.

By 1960, William Prosser argued that privacy in tort law was recognized by an overwhelming number of American courts. He described the law of privacy as comprising four distinct kinds of tort invasion:

(1) intrusion upon the plaintiff's seclusion or solitude, or into his private affairs

(2) public disclosure of embarrassing private facts about the plaintiff

(3) publicity that places the plaintiff in a false light in the public eye

(4) appropriation, for the defendant's advantage, of the plaintiff's name or likeness[26]

Prosser's four-part interest analysis was then incorporated into the Second Restatement of Torts, and both became influential for the courts.

But Prosser's is not the only theoretical interpretation of privacy protection in tort law. In 1964, Dean Edward J. Bloustein contended in a *New York University Law Review* article that Prosser's description was inadequate and conceptually thin.[27] Bloustein argued, in reply to Prosser, that protection of informational privacy in tort law formed a unitary concept, which he described as protection for individual liberty to do as we will and protection from the affront to human dignity occurring when individuals and government invade our privacy. On Bloustein's view, the emotional distress felt is a consequence of a loss of privacy and can be used as a measure for damages, but the fundamental basis of the legal injury in tort, Fourth Amendment, and related cases is the affront to human dignity.

Tort rights are generally held by individuals against private persons or businesses. Rights of individuals against intrusion by the government are protected as constitutional rights. While some commentators have viewed the protection of informational privacy in tort law as distinct from privacy protection under the Fourth and Fifth Amendments to the Constitution, the more common and reasonable view is to recognize the link between them. The values underlying protection against unreasonable search and seizure and protection from self-incrimination clearly include the need to control access to and information about oneself.

Fourth Amendment proscriptions against unreasonable searches and seizures obviously protect such interests as property and freedom of the press, in addition to privacy. But the Supreme Court has been explicit in ruling that privacy is a central reason for Fourth Amendment limitations on governmental searches. The earliest constitutional challenges to federal law tied privacy interests to physical control over a dwelling or other property seized as a tangible item. For example, in *Ex parte Jackson* in 1877, the Supreme Court held that a sealed letter entrusted to the mail is subject to Fourth Amendment warrant requirements,[28] and in *Boyd v. United States* in 1886 held that a person's private papers were protected from seizure by the Fourth and Fifth Amendments.[29] Because the Fourth Amendment language refers specifically to private papers of the sort protected in *Jackson*, the question later arose whether the amendment also gave protection from electronic surveillance by the government.

In *Olmstead v. United States* in 1928 the Court majority held that conversations over the telephone were not covered by Fourth Amendment protection, on the grounds that there was no entry, no search, and no seizure in overhearing them.[30] Justice Brandeis's famous dissent pointed out that changes over time make it possible for government to use more subtle and far-reaching means of invading privacy. Even without removing papers from drawers, he argued, government can gain access to them and reproduce them. Consequently, a telephone message over public telephone lines must be viewed as essentially no different from a sealed letter in the public mail. Both deserve Fourth Amendment protection. He argued,

The makers of our Constitution undertook to secure conditions favorable to the pursuit of happiness. They recognized the significance of man's spiritual nature, of his feelings and of his intellect. They knew that only a part of the pain, pleasure and satisfaction of life are to be found in material things. They sought to protect Americans in their beliefs, their thoughts, their emotions and their sensations. They conferred, as against the government, the right to be let alone—the most comprehensive of rights and the right most valued by civilized men. To protect that right, every unjustifiable intrusion by the government upon the privacy of the individual, whatever the means employed, must be deemed a violation of the 4th Amendment.[31]

Clearly it is not the type of injurer, either a private party or government, that is relevant here, but the nature of the injury, the intrusion on one's privacy.

It is interesting to note that nowhere in his *Olmstead* dissent did Brandeis refer to the earlier article he and Warren had written. But as Bloustein has pointed out, the structure of his argument in *Olmstead* was parallel to that of the article, and several passages from the essay were included almost verbatim in the Brandeis dissent in *Olmstead.*[32]

By the time the Supreme Court decided *Berger v. New York*[33] and *Katz v. United States*[34] in 1967, extending Fourth Amendment protection to conversations overheard by wiretap and transmission eavesdropping, the majority recognized the seriousness of the privacy threat posed by electronic surveillance that Brandeis had noted forty years earlier. Such surveillance can interfere with one's solitude, intimacy, anonymity, and ability to control dispersal of information. Beyond this, Alan Westin has argued, undesired revelations can undermine one's "personal autonomy," one's "individuality," and one's dignity and worth as a human being by penetrating the privacy of one's "core self," leaving one exposed to ridicule and shame, and under the control of others who know one's secrets.[35]

The majority of the Court held that Charles Katz had a justified expectation of privacy in his telephone conversation despite its taking place in a public phone booth. In this case the Supreme Court expanded its interpretation by ruling that the Fourth Amendment protects people, not places. In his concurring opinion, Justice Harlan articulated a two-part requirement for determining a governmental Fourth Amendment search violation: (i) that a person demonstrate an actual (subjective) expectation of privacy and (ii) that the expectation be one that society is willing to recognize as "reasonable." With subsequent modification and refinement concerning what constitutes a "legitimate expectation of privacy" and what can defeat it (voluntary disclosure, for example),[36] this test has continued to dominate Fourth Amendment privacy protection cases. The test is not unproblematic, however, and has repeatedly generated controversy within Fourth Amendment jurisprudence.[37]

What I am referring to as "tort privacy" now covers interests individuals have in protection from unwarranted searches or observations of themselves and their activities, materials, and conversations, whether these occur in person or through electronic surveillance. Owing to the growth of computer technology and capacities for the rapid recording and retrieval of vast amounts of data, protection has also been increased against having one's communications reproduced or misused without authorization and against having information about oneself appropriated and exploited. Such abuse of information includes attacks on one's reputation, disclosure of embarrassing facts, and use of one's name or likeness without permission. Alternatively, the protected data may be relevant to the Privacy Act of 1974, which covers employment, academic, and medical records; for example, the act blocks the use of social security records in determining eligibility for the draft. Most recently the Court has addressed and debated more complex cases involving nonconsensual disclosure of telephone numbers; telephone, bank, credit card, and credit bureau records; involuntary polygraph tests; school searches; blood, urine, breath, and HIV tests; eavesdropping over cellular phones; and video surveillance. In later chapters, I shall discuss the privacy concerns arising in some of these contexts in more detail.

In many of the more recent privacy cases there has been a shift away from reasoning that takes a rights-oriented approach toward more arguments that use a utilitarian cost-benefit analysis, which balances the costs to privacy and the benefits to public safety and crime control.[38] Despite this shift in reasoning, the clear trend has been the expansion of privacy rights, not the reverse. The proliferation of privacy rights is evident in federal cases, in state constitutions, and in federal law. "In fact," writes Richard Posner, "the legislative trend is toward giving individuals more and more privacy protection with respect to facts and communications, and business firms and other organizations (including government agencies, universities, and hospitals) less and less."[39]

Beginning in 1965, the Supreme Court also recognized an apparently distinct constitutional right to privacy independent of the Fourth Amendment. Because there is no right to privacy explicitly guaranteed in the Constitution, and because the constitutional cases invoking this right are so diverse, there has been a great deal of criticism and controversy surrounding this constitutional right to privacy. It is even more difficult to describe than the informational privacy protected in tort and Fourth Amendment law. This second legal right was first recognized and announced by the Supreme Court in *Griswold v. Connecticut* when the Court overturned convictions of the director of Planned Parenthood in Connecticut and a doctor from Yale Medical School for violating a statute that banned disbursement of contraceptive-related information, instruction, and medical advice to married persons.[40]

Controversy began almost immediately because there were four opinions written in defense of the judgment, each offering a different justification.

In his opinion for the Court, Justice William O. Douglas defended a "penumbral" right to privacy "emanating" from the Constitution and its amendments. According to Douglas, this right protected a "zone" of privacy, including both the intimate relation of husband and wife and their physician's role with respect to that relation. This zone of privacy covering the sexual relationship of married persons was, Douglas argued, protected by several fundamental guarantees. Douglas might have grounded *Griswold* solely on Fourth Amendment protection, arguing that enforcement of the statute would violate privacy by requiring searches of bedrooms and surveillance of intimate activities. He chose, however, to defend the social institution of marriage using a broader argument, citing the First Amendment freedom to teach and give information, Third Amendment protection of one's home, and Fifth Amendment protection against self-incrimination, in addition to Fourth Amendment protection of the security of one's person, home, papers, and effects. All, he argued, showed the privacy right at stake in *Griswold* to be a legitimate one compatible with our constitutional history. He stated in conclusion, "We deal with a right of privacy older than the Bill of Rights, older than our political parties, older than our school system."

There are historical connections between privacy and First Amendment values.[41] Moreover, it is interesting to note that Douglas's now well-known argument linking the group of several amendments was not new or unique to the *Griswold* case. Other commentators have pointed out that

An often quoted statement from Justice Douglas links not only the first, fourth, and fifth amendments but ties values reflected in these amendments to the role of the Constitution and individual rights in protecting human dignity. "These three amendments are indeed closely related, safeguarding not only privacy and protection against self-incrimination,

but 'conscience and human dignity and freedom of expression as well.' "
Frank v. Maryland, 359 U.S. 350, 376 (1959) (Douglas, J., dissenting).[42]

In reviewing the multiple appeals made by Douglas in *Griswold,* it is worth emphasizing the similarities between his arguments and those made in *Pavesich v. New England Life Insurance Company.* As described earlier, *Pavesich* was the first case to recognize privacy as a right in tort law by invoking natural law, common law, and constitutional values. It is now possible to see how the *Griswold* arguments were anticipated in *Pavesich,* providing a natural basis for connecting the two cases.

Others on the *Griswold* Court were unpersuaded by Douglas's arguments. They thought the decision should be justified by the due process clause or the concept of liberty of the Fourteenth Amendment, or by the Ninth Amendment, which states, "The enumeration in the Constitution, of certain rights, shall not be construed to deny or disparage others retained by the people."[43] The idea behind this latter argument may have been that the writers of the Constitution deemed privacy protection for marital relations so clearly beyond the province of governmental regulation that there was no need to stipulate it explicitly. The influence on the framers of Puritan religious beliefs lends support to this explanation.

Soon after the *Griswold* decision, the right to privacy was cited in *Loving v. Virginia* as justification to overturn a Virginia statute against interracial marriage,[44] in *Stanley v. Georgia* as one major reason for allowing "possession of obscene matter" in one's home,[45] and in *Eisenstadt v. Baird* as the reason to allow distribution of contraceptive devices. Justice Brennan wrote in *Eisenstadt,* "if the right of privacy means anything, it is the right of the *individual,* married or single, to be free from unwarranted governmental intrusion into matters so fundamentally affecting a person as the decision whether to bear or beget a child."[46] Thus the Court recognized the importance of privacy for individuals, married or not. This paved the way for using the constitutional right to privacy as a defense for the famous and controversial *Roe v.*

Wade abortion decision the following year.[47] Then in *Moore v. City of East Cleveland* privacy was extended to decisions concerning family composition and living arrangements.[48] The constitutional privacy right is also associated by scholars and judges with earlier decisions that struck down a law requiring students to be educated at public schools,[49] and banned Oklahoma's statute providing for mandatory sterilization of recidivists convicted of three felonies.[50]

Although the constitutional right to privacy played a central role in *Roe v. Wade* and subsequent decisions on third-party consent for abortions for minors,[51] it has been less successful in protecting funding for abortions[52] and protecting father's rights,[53] protecting computer records of patients who have prescriptions for dangerous but lawful drugs,[54] and protecting the privacy of intimate sexual behavior in *Bowers v. Hardwick*.[55]

Many commentators have defined the tort interest in privacy as "control over information about oneself," and that interest is referred to as the classic notion or core of privacy. Given this intuitive characterization of tort and Fourth Amendment privacy concerns, it is possible to see a conceptual difference between privacy interests protected in tort and Fourth Amendment law and constitutional privacy. Paradigmatically, tort privacy cases involve concerns with information—either conveyed by an individual (e.g. in private conversation or activity) or about an individual (e.g., records, newspaper stories)—or with an individual's likeness. We should take care to note, however, that tort privacy is not as univocal as this description indicates. In tort and Fourth Amendment law, intrusive behavior such as snooping or spying can violate privacy even if no information is gathered or disseminated.

The constitutional privacy right has continued to be elusive. The Court was divided on its original justification, and Douglas's majority opinion has invited criticism: in part because of his use of vague terms such as "zone," "emanating," and "penumbral," and in part because of his appeals to so many constitutional amendments in defense of the right. In addition, the diversity of claims subsequently protected under the term "privacy," ranging over issues related to one's body, family relations, lifestyle, and child rearing, has contributed to making constitutional privacy vulnerable to attack.

In 1977, in *Whalen v. Roe*, the Court made its most comprehensive effort thus far to define the right to privacy, embracing both (i) an "individual interest in avoiding disclosure of personal matters" and (ii) an "interest in independence in making certain kinds of important decisions."[56] The case was deemed to involve both aspects of privacy. Nevertheless, the Court upheld New York statutes that mandate centralized computer records of prescriptions for certain dangerous but lawful drugs such as opium derivatives and amphetamines, even though the records included the patients' names and addresses. The Court argued that careful security provisions in the law showed "proper concern" for privacy protection and that there was no justification for assuming the provisions would not be administered properly. It argued, moreover, that no patient was denied either access to the drugs under consideration or the right to decide, independently with his or her physician, to use any of the medications.[57] It is surprising that the full Court did not recognize the concerns generated by a readily available computerized file to be a serious enough threat to privacy to strike down the statute. Indeed, in his concurrence, Justice Brennan found the easy accessibility of computerized data particularly troubling, and he indicated that future developments might demonstrate the necessity for placing curbs on such technology.

Given the two-pronged characterization of privacy expressed by the Court in *Whalen*, as well as the historical development of two sets of privacy cases, it is hardly surprising that what I have been calling the tort interest in privacy (which still arises, of course, in Supreme Court cases) and the constitutional right to privacy (now often cited in lower court decisions) are often viewed as separable interests. I shall argue, however, that there are more similarities between these interests than are usually acknowledged.

T W O

Narrow Views of Privacy
Developed from the Law

My overall concern is the realm of the private. My goals in this chapter are to criticize narrow views of privacy developed in the law and to highlight similarities between tort, Fourth Amendment, and other constitutional privacy interests, in order to establish the need for developing a broader conception of privacy. I shall focus on a prevalent line of argument concerning ambiguities surrounding the historical divergence between privacy protection developed in tort and constitutional law. William Parent, Louis Henkin, John Hart Ely, and others argue that the term "privacy" can be used legitimately only to describe protection over information and knowledge about oneself; they also argue that despite the Supreme Court's reliance on a right to privacy, the constitutional cases are concerned solely with an interest in autonomy or liberty in some sense.[1]

In demonstrating that such characterizations of privacy are conceptually thin and do not adequately account for many common intuitions about privacy, I focus particularly on Parent's influential narrow definition of privacy and on Henkin's version of the argument that the constitutional cases since *Griswold v. Connecticut*[2] invoking a right to privacy are "spurious" privacy cases because the central concept involved is autonomy or liberty. Despite Parent's defense of this view, the recognition that a notion of privacy is relevant in the constitutional line of cases since *Griswold* need not lead us to conflate privacy and liberty. It is now clear that there is some intuitive difference between the "tort" and "constitutional" privacy interests. But I argue that the constitutional cases cannot all be adequately characterized as protecting merely an "autonomy" interest, providing an alternative explanation of the relationship between privacy and autonomy which is plausible and shows that even when autonomy is involved, the constitutional cases *can* be understood to raise important privacy issues.

Two points should be kept in mind. First, throughout my discussion I shall not place special weight on privacy as a right, as opposed to a claim or interest. A "claim" is often described as an argument that someone deserves something. A "right" is then a justified claim: justified by laws or judicial decisions if it is a legal right, by moral principles if it is a moral right.[3] However, I am making moral and legal points that are significant independently of whether or not we can ultimately make sense of rights, explain when they are binding, or show they are reducible to utilitarian claims. Since the literature on privacy uses rights terminology I must accommodate that. But because I am making no claim about a theory of rights, whenever possible I shall refer to privacy as an "interest" (which can be invaded), by which I mean something it would be a good thing to have, leaving open the question of how extensively it ought to be protected.

Second, nothing in my discussion requires assuming that one endorse all the decisions in cases I cite. One need not accept the actual rulings to inquire whether the diverse privacy claims are related. Indeed, dissent is likely for at least two reasons: (i) the concept of privacy has been so poorly articulated that it is not clear what is protected and what is not and (ii) even a clearer understanding of the range of concerns that are private will not dictate how privacy should be balanced against other individual rights or public concerns. One may have an important interest in privacy that for legal or social reasons cannot be protected.

Parent on Privacy and the Public Record

Understanding William Parent's reasonable but inadequate position will provide a helpful way of addressing more general issues about privacy's scope and meaning. Motivated by a concern to provide a definition of privacy that (i) "is by and large consistent with ordinary language" and (ii) does "not usurp or encroach upon the basic meanings and functions" of other related concepts, Parent defines privacy as "the condition of not having undocumented personal information [knowledge] about oneself known [possessed] by others."[4] He stresses that he is defining the "condition" of privacy as opposed to the right to privacy. The difference, he explains, is that the condition of privacy is a moral value for persons who also prize freedom and individuality; part of its defense against unwarranted invasion should include advocacy of a moral right to privacy. This moral right is in turn protected by law, and on Parent's view it should be guaranteed more fully than it is at present. The distinction is important because it allows us to acknowledge that diminishing privacy need not violate a moral or legal right to privacy, and vice versa.

The terms of Parent's definition are significant. "Personal" knowledge is, according to Parent, knowledge of personal information. Such information must be factual, he believes, because making public falsehoods or subjective opinions does not constitute an invasion of privacy; it is appropriately characterized as slander, libel, or defamation. Furthermore, information that is personal consists either of facts that most persons in a given society choose not to reveal about themselves (except to close friends, family, etc.) or of facts about which a particular individual is acutely sensitive and which he or she therefore does not choose to reveal, even though most people do not care if similar facts are widely known about themselves. Thus in our culture facts about sexual orientations, salaries, physical or mental health, and so on are examples of personal information. Even such matters as height or marital status can be instances of personal information for individuals sensitive to these facts. Finally, personal information is "documented" only in the case that it belongs to the public record: that is, it can be found in newspapers, court proceedings, and other official documents available to the public.[5] This characterization is meant to exclude information about individuals kept on file for a particular purpose, such as medical or employment records, which are not available for public perusal.

A valuable feature of Parent's account is that he not only sees privacy as a coherent concept but also takes the view that there is something unique, fundamental, and of special value in it. In contrast, "reductionists" such as Judith Thomson have argued that the right to privacy is not an independent right but is "derivative" from other rights, most notably property rights and rights to bodily security.[6] Commentators taking this approach differ, of course, yet all agree that talk of privacy as an independent notion will not be illuminating.[7] By considering Thomson's examples in detail, Parent shows that it is surely *as* plausible that the reverse of reductionism is true, that other rights such as those of ownership or rights over one's person are "derivative" from privacy rights.[8] Indeed this is likely if there is a distinctive and important value designated by the term "privacy." A second strength of Parent's approach is the extent to which he recognizes and accommodates the fact that privacy is a conventional or relative notion. Because what counts as personal information may vary from group to group or individual to individual, and may change over time, there is no fixed realm of the private. This relativist feature of privacy is well known but not often emphasized. Nevertheless, it must be allowed for by any adequate account.[9]

In attempting to isolate the conceptual core of privacy, Parent is right to be dissatisfied with Judge Cooley's famous but overbroad characterization of privacy as a right "to be let alone."[10] Yet he overreacts in the opposite direction and defends a definition of privacy that is much too narrow. Consider first Parent's emphasis on *undocumented* personal knowledge. We can imagine a case in which personal information about some individual has become part of the public record through a violation of privacy. A news agency, for example, surreptitiously taps an entertainer's telephone and subsequently publishes revealing information about that person's sex life or drug use. Given Parent's definition of privacy, once that information becomes part of the public record there is no violation of privacy in repeated publication of the information. The entertainer has no recourse for future protection; the information is no longer private even if the original disclosure was an error or a moral wrong.

In defense of his view, Parent says, "What belongs to the public domain cannot without glaring paradox be called private and consequently should not be incorporated within a viable conception of privacy."[11] If the original publication surfaced in a nationally syndicated daily, subsequent publication might seem only mildly invasive. But if the first disclosure occurred in publicly accessible but obscure documents, it is difficult to deny that a widely distributed reprint would be a further intrusion on the individual's privacy. The general point is that we are not likely to view perpetrating a violation as any less of a violation just because the agent is not the first one to invade the other's privacy. For example, during former Massachusetts Representative Margaret Heckler's divorce proceedings, her husband claimed they had not had sexual relations in twenty years. Although this information was publicly available to reporters in the courtroom, it seems clear that the subsequent media coverage not only diminished Heckler's privacy but also violated her right to privacy.

Parent replies that similar publicity in the case of a rape victim cannot be condemned on privacy grounds; instead, it should be criticized because it abridges her anonymity. It is far from clear that his account reflects our ordinary linguistic usage or is even applicable to Heckler's case. And even if we did talk of a "right to anonymity" in certain instances, surely it would be accorded to the victim so that her privacy would not be invaded. Indeed, there are legal counterexamples to Parent's position.[12] Yet on Parent's account, once information becomes part of the public record, whether legitimately or not, further release of it never invades privacy.

Moreover, if any personal information is part of the public record, then even the most insidious snooping to attain that information does not constitute a privacy intrusion. There is no invasion of privacy as long as "the information revealed was publicly available and could have been found out by anyone, without resort to snooping or prying."[13] Parent's test depends solely on whether or not the personal information is part of the public domain. Yet most of us would find that snooping diminishes our privacy, even if done by someone unaware that the facts in question were already documented. To be sure, snooping, spying, and other methods of acquisition are not always determinative of a privacy invasion. For example, I may intrude on another's privacy by overhearing a quiet conversation on a subway. Nevertheless, the mode of acquisition cannot be said to be irrelevant, as Parent's account of privacy suggests it may be.

These considerations introduce a more general concern. Parent has identified privacy invasions with possession of undocumented personal information, but he has provided no way of judging what should or should not be a part of the public record. His descriptive emphasis on what is *as a matter of fact* part of the public record leaves no room for a normative sense of privacy encompassing interests *worthy* of protection.[14] Consider, for example, Blue Cross/Blue Shield guidelines that have recently been revised so that for psychological or psychiatric as well as physical treatment, specific descriptions of the ailment being treated are required in order for patients to receive reimbursement. While the Privacy Act of 1974 protects the content of medical and other records, if these detailed descriptions should be deemed necessary as public verification of the legitimacy of any payments, they will not be private given Parent's definition. Thus by this account, even very personal information can, through legislative action or decisions by agencies requiring its release, become "nonprivate" by virtue of its becoming documented. The question of what it is legitimate for the public to know is never addressed.

A second question we can ask is why Parent characterizes privacy as the condition of not having undocumented personal *knowledge* about one possessed by others. One problem is that it may be difficult to determine the truth of some statements. More important we may still ask why knowledge must be disseminated for there to be a loss of privacy. Parent states, "Invasion of privacy must consist of truthful disclosures about a person. . . . [P]rivacy is invaded by certain kinds of intrusions, namely those of a cognitive nature that *result in the acquisition* of undocumented personal facts" (emphasis mine).[15] It is never clear whether it is the acquisition or the disclosure of information that troubles Parent most deeply. But what if there is neither? If one secretly trains a telescope on another but discovers nothing that is not already public information, has there been no privacy invasion? Consider Parent's discussion of an example of Thomson's: a great opera singer, who no longer wants to be listened to, only sings quietly behind soundproof walls. If she is nonetheless heard through an ingenious and strategically placed amplifier, what knowledge about her is gained? Even if none, most of us would agree there has been a privacy invasion. Parent himself seems confused on such cases. In assessing this example he writes, "If B's snooping is without justification it should be condemned as a violation of A's right to privacy,"[16] indicating that the unjustified spying itself, independent of any knowledge acquired, is determinative of a privacy violation. The problem then reduces to when such snooping is justified and when it is not. Yet according to Parent's definition we must agree that there have been no privacy invasions in cases where no undocumented personal facts become known.

We might make sense of his remarks by requiring such information acquisition only for a loss of privacy, not for a violation of a right. Yet this is not Parent's reply, and he instead invites us to apply his test to determine whether privacy is diminished as a legal standard, presumably relevant for determining rights violations as well. He does suggest an alternative response, however: namely, that knowledge *is* gained in many such cases. The snooper with the telescope sees the person's posture and attire, for example, and the eavesdropper hears what the opera singer sings, how often, and so on. Nevertheless, with repeated observations it is less clear that *new* knowledge is gained. And when the information is trivial we have good reason to doubt that the knowledge gained helps explain *why* we consider privacy the issue. Parent concedes, moreover, that if one snoops and fails to gather information, then there is no privacy invasion although the action is condemnable as unwarranted trespass. But then if the singer is practicing in a building owned by a third party, the most he can claim is that the snooper committed a wrong against the owner, not the singer! If he tries to say there is a sense in which the listener does trespass against the singer, then "trespass" is merely standing in for a certain kind of privacy invasion, whether he admits it or not.

Third, even if we weaken Parent's definition so that we do not always require that knowledge be gained for privacy to be invaded, we may wonder why it is reasonable to focus on possession of *information* as central to privacy.[17] If privacy is merely the condition of not having others possess certain information, it appears that privacy is tantamount to secrecy. Yet Parent explicitly denies he is making such an identification, and for good reason. Historically, protection of information has been prominent but not exhaustive in the development of privacy law. As we have seen, Warren and Brandeis first sought protection from publication, without consent or adequate justification, not only of personal information but also of one's name or likeness. The Fourth and Fifth Amendment protections against unreasonable search and seizures and self-incrimination prohibit potentially oppressive governmental surveillance as well as information gathering. They now limit wiretapping and other forms of electronic eavesdropping in addition to the physical intrusions on privacy that were once their primary target.[18]

Moreover, it is widely recognized that others' physical access to one can limit one's privacy in other ways as well. Ruth Gavison has argued that one can lose privacy merely by becoming the object of attention, even if no new information becomes known and whether the attention is conscious and purposeful, or inadvertent.[19] More obviously, individuals' privacy is diminished when others gain physical proximity to them—as Peeping Toms, for example—by observation of their bodies, behavior, or interactions; by entry into a home under false pretenses; or even by a move from a single-person office to a shared one. In none of these cases it is necessary for new information to be acquired for there to be a privacy intrusion.

There are other examples to counter Parent's argument. Consider a man who knows his wife's body very well but is now divorced from her and spying on her as she takes a bath.[20] It is difficult to deny that her privacy is being invaded. Thomas Scanlon makes the general point graphically: "If you press personal questions on me in a situation in which this is conventionally forbidden, I can always refuse to answer. But the *fact that no information is revealed* does not remove the violation, which remains just as does the analogous violation when you peek through my bathroom window but fail to see me because I have taken some mildly inconvenient evasive action."[21] Parent responds that privacy is irrelevant in such cases. At worst there is harassment (and possibly trespass).

Parent's general strategy, then, in cases where no new information is acquired, is to urge that while there *is* a violation, it is unrelated to privacy—it constitutes either abridgment of anonymity (rape victim), trespass (insidious snooping, as the opera singer suffers), or harassment (Scanlon's case). But as an argument for a conclusion about privacy, this hardly suffices. That an act involves harassment, trespass, or infringes one's anonymity implies nothing whatsoever about whether or not it also diminishes or violates one's privacy.[22] At best, Parent captures some of the legal extension of the concept of privacy, not the nature of our moral notion of privacy. Hence we must reject information acquisition and publication as solely determinative of privacy invasions. If we do so, and acknowledge that privacy concerns encompass not only information but actions and physical access as well, then we have good reason to consider a broader view that extends the realm of the private to include the sort of multiple privacy interests protected in constitutional law as well as those associated with tort law.

Henkin on Privacy and Autonomy

Consider next arguments concerning the constitutional privacy cases. Since it was first posited the constitutional right to privacy has been severely criticized. It has been called "pernicious," "a malformation of constitutional law which thrives because of the conceptual vacuum surrounding the legal notions of privacy," and "a composite term whose sense is illusory."[23] There is general worry that the right flagrantly expresses subjective judicial ideology and is a form of legislative policy making not properly a function of the courts, because there is no explicit passage in the Constitution or Bill of Rights mentioning or justifying the right as described by the Court. Worse still, while other legal rights (such as the right to travel from state to state) are not mentioned in the Constitution, they are plausibly inferable in some way. But the constitutional right to privacy, it is claimed, cannot be inferred from the intent of the framers or from the governmental system depicted by the Constitution.

There is also a philosophically more important claim which I wish here to address: namely, that the constitutional cases relying on *Griswold* involve rights that have "no basis in any meaningful conception of privacy."[24] According to John Hart Ely, privacy involves concealment, and in *Roe v. Wade*, for example, "the court neither provides an alternative definition [of privacy] nor an account of why *it* thinks privacy is involved."[25] One argument for this claim urges that the tort and constitutional privacy cases rest on two distinct concepts. On this view, a great deal of confusion can be resolved if we recognize that interests traditionally protected in tort law and under the Fourth Amendment as privacy interests can be identified as genuine privacy issues. Yet the line of constitutional cases developed from *Griswold*, despite Supreme Court declarations to the contrary, are not about privacy at all; instead, they are concerned solely with an interest in "autonomy" or "liberty" in some sense. Louis Henkin observes,

It has been insufficiently noticed that what the Court has been talking about is not at all what most people mean by privacy. None of the recent cases, and none of the older cases the Court cited (except those dealing with search and seizure under the Fourth Amendment), which the Justices have now swept together into the basket labeled "right of privacy," deals with any of the matters that are the subject of the now massive literature on privacy. In *Griswold, Baird, Wade,* and *Stanley,* the Court was not talking about my freedom from official intrusion into my home, my person, my papers, my telephone; about my right to be free from official surveillance or accosting, from questions by census takers, officials, congressional bodies, forms and returns containing information of varying degrees of "privateness"; from being mentioned and publicized, or having data about me collected. . . . In a word, the Court has been vindicating not a right to freedom from official intrusion, but to freedom from official regulation.

It is this latter freedom that Henkin calls "autonomy." He continues,

That the Court cites search and seizure cases as precedent for its new zone of autonomy suggests that it does not distinguish between privacy and autonomy and may be treating them both as aspects of "the right to be let alone." But they are, I think, different notions conceptually, with different philosophical, political, social (and, one might have thought, legal) assumptions and consequences; they may look different also if viewed as aspects of the confrontation of private right with public good.[26]

Henkin makes several claims in this passage that we can readily endorse. No one would dispute that based on traditional characterizations of privacy and autonomy, the two notions are differentiable, and we can agree we ought not to confuse them. Moreover, "freedom from official intrusion" may surely be shown to differ from "freedom from official regulation." It is somewhat less clear that there are distinguishable and apparently unrelated sets of cases protected under the term "privacy." Henkin refers to privacy protection developed previous to the constitutional privacy right as "hard-core" privacy, and he has surely overemphasized *official* intrusions in his description of it. Tort law privacy protection over information often shields one from invasions by other individuals. Nevertheless, his most troubling claim is that our common notion of privacy encompasses only these hard-core interests and that the constitutional cases relying on *Griswold* can be said to involve "autonomy" alone and to have no relation to an interesting or important conception of privacy.

To understand the problem, we might first examine the notion of autonomy that is supposed to characterize these constitutional cases. Henkin tells us that by autonomy he means "freedom from governmental regulation." Unfortunately, this definition leaves it unclear why a "new" zone of autonomy is protected. There seems to be nothing about the contraception, abortion, or pornography cases, for example, that distinguishes them from all other cases where state regulation is involved. Yet the Court has made it clear that whatever is covered by the privacy right is something other than the totality of acts or decisions left unregulated by government. Henkin's definition is so broad that it fails to explain why these constitutional cases stand apart in their protection of autonomy under the term "privacy" and why the Court attaches special importance to them. Indeed, it is difficult to discern from Henkin's discussion why "autonomy" is a more appropriate term than the classic "negative liberty" for his concept of freedom from regulation.[27] It is thus interesting that William Parent has recently given a version of Henkin's argument in terms of "liberty," an argument we shall consider below.

It has been suggested that by itself, the concept of negative freedom is empty. If a person is objectively free from coercion but lacks the capacities of rational self-direction or self-control, then there is an important sense in which we can say that person is not free.[28] Thus we might alternatively take Henkin's notion of autonomy to mean not merely freedom from governmental regulation but also the capacity for individual control over certain aspects of one's life. Recall, however, that Henkin is concerned to differentiate constitutional from tort and Fourth Amendment privacy cases as protecting distinct types of claims resting on different concepts. But if the constitutional cases are based on autonomy as individual control, then this concept *relates*, rather than differentiates, the constitutional interest in privacy and the tort interest in "control over information about oneself." Both types of cases can be said to involve individual control, in distinction to control by others. And again, this seems to be the issue in nearly every legal dispute, so we have no criterion for setting apart the constitutional privacy cases.

Perhaps Henkin's point is that the constitutional privacy cases ought not be distinguished in any special way. Nevertheless, there is a further problem. Critics of the Court's use of a constitutional right to privacy—those who believe the cases involve solely a notion of liberty or autonomy and no genuine privacy concerns—do not agree on the ultimate constitutional justifiability of the cases. Ely argues, for example, that there is no constitutional basis in liberty for the *Roe* decision, nor does he believe *any other* constitutional justification is possible. Henkin, in contrast, thinks the "Court's creation of an additional zone of individual autonomy . . . does not . . . clearly exceed the bounds of judicial innovation."[29] Even if the Court failed to give an adequate justification, Henkin believes the constitutional privacy decisions *could* be defended by using the a priori notion of autonomy in line with our country's original philosophy, though unwritten in the Constitution; or by relying on autonomy implied in the Ninth Amendment and incorporated in the Fourteenth; or by a return to substantive due process.[30] Thus simply reclassifying the constitutional right to privacy as a liberty or autonomy interest leaves unresolved the question of whether or not those constitutional judgments can be justified.

An alternative way of distinguishing tort privacy and the constitutional privacy cases has been suggested by Thomas Huff. On his view the former is an "interest in being free of the potential for certain unwarranted evaluations," whereas what he calls "constitutional autonomy" is an interest in being kept free from state interference in making certain particularly intimate and personal choices.[31] This suggests that we might more reasonably distinguish the constitutional privacy interests in terms of a notion of autonomy somewhat different from Henkin's and philosophically more familiar, a notion more Kantian in that it focuses on an individual's capacity to choose and be "self-legislative." Such a concept also comes close to the Court's own characterization of the constitutional aspect of privacy in *Whalen*.[32]

This is a much more plausible sense of autonomy to ascribe to the constitutional privacy cases. After all, one *chooses* to get contraceptive information and devices, *chooses* a marriage partner, *chooses* to have an abortion, and *chooses* to read pornography at home. But it does not seem to distinguish those cases from the tort privacy cases in the way Henkin had hoped.[33] For the goal in many of the latter is to ensure one's *choice* of who should have what information about oneself, one's *choice* that written or verbal communications not be made public, that one's likeness not be used without one's permission, that one's records and professional relationships be kept confidential, and so on. Individual choice about basic matters in one's life may well be central, but this feature also appears to relate rather than differentiate the constitutional right to privacy and the tort interest in privacy. Yet at least one difference emerges. Choices in the constitutional cases appear in general to be positive choices, or decisions to act or behave in certain ways, whereas those in tort cases are generally negative choices, or choices that others ought to refrain or forbear from acting in certain ways. It is not clear that this difference coincides with the distinction between tort and constitutional privacy claims in every instance. To the extent that it does hold, however, it can at best support an argument about when *autonomy* is relevant. It implies nothing whatsoever about the range of cases in which *privacy* is a central concern.

It is worth digressing to note that two other initially plausible ways of distinguishing tort and constitutional privacy ultimately indicate similarities between those interests. First, in constitutional privacy cases a legal right is generally asserted against the government not to intrude on or regulate one in a certain way, whereas in tort cases the claim may be against a particular individual,[34] a group such as a news agency,[35] or against the state.[36] And Fourth Amendment protection against unreasonable searches and seizures in "persons, houses, papers, and effects," while generally upheld for individuals against improper invasions by the government or its representatives, has in the literature been associated closely with tort protection, since both often shield personal papers, documents, and other similar effects. Thus isolating whether the right is against an individual (*in personam*), against the world at large (*in rem*), or against the government does not adequately differentiate between the tort or Fourth Amendment and the constitutional privacy claims.

A second way of capturing what many see as a clear distinction between the two legal interests in privacy focuses on paradigmatic cases that illustrate a difference between emotional and physical harm. After all, Warren and Brandeis were concerned in part that individuals be protected from mental distress resulting from the publication of their correspondence or of information about them. They appeared to focus on preserving peace of mind, whereas defending access to contraception or abortion assures types of protection for the body. But a distinction between mental and physical protection cannot possibly be an acceptable way of differentiating tort and constitutional privacy interests. Contraception and abortion regulations have major psychological consequences, and decisions about whether one can read pornography at home or how one must educate one's children help determine the limits of the government to homogenize or affect the beliefs and attitudes of the populace. On the other side, tort law has expanded privacy protection far beyond what Warren and Brandeis originally argued for. Physical harassment by bill collectors, photographers, or the press are now considered invasions of privacy in tort law, and intrusions to get information about individuals may be extremely physical when they involve planting a recording device, a bodily search, blood tests, or even stomach pumping. Thus in tort and Fourth Amendment law as well as in constitutional law, privacy protects both peace of mind and bodily integrity.[37]

Let us return, then, to the sense of autonomy attributed to moral agents not subject to the will of others that *does* appear relevant to the constitutional privacy cases: the capacity to make independent and self-legislating choices. We can agree that this autonomy is involved in the constitutional privacy cases—and many other cases as well—*without denying* that privacy is also crucial. It is clear, then, that a more intuitive explanation than Henkin's allows that privacy and autonomy are distinct though related concepts. Many privacy issues, such as protection from unwarranted electronic surveillance, will have nothing to do with autonomous decision making. Conversely, many self-determined choices—to drive with car stereo blaring through a quiet neighborhood, for example—can be made by an individual but will not in any further sense be private decisions; thus privacy is not involved. However, a subset of autonomous decisions, certain personal decisions regarding one's basic lifestyle, can be said to involve privacy interests. They should be viewed as autonomy cases in virtue of their concern with individual, as opposed to state, decision-making *power*; and privacy is at stake because the *nature* of the decision is crucial to one's "inviolate personality" or bodily integrity. It is no conflation of concepts to say that a particular act is both a theft and a trespass. Similarly, acknowledging that there is both an invasion of privacy and a violation of autonomy in a given case need not confuse those concepts.

Privacy and Liberty

In an argument reminiscent of Henkin's, Parent continues his defense of a narrow definition of privacy. He objects to an account of privacy relevant to the constitutional cases, which he describes as "control over significant personal matters," on the grounds that it is based on a conceptual error: confusing privacy and liberty. He argues,

The defining idea of liberty is the absence of external restraints or coercion. A person who is behind bars or locked in a room or physically pinned to the ground is unfree to do many things. Similarly, a person who is prohibited by law from making certain choices should be described as having been denied the liberty or freedom to make them. The loss of liberty in these cases takes the form of a deprivation of autonomy. Hence we can meaningfully say that the right to liberty embraces in part the right of persons to make fundamentally important choices about their

lives and therewith to exercise significant control over different aspects
of their behavior. It is clearly distinguishable from the right to privacy,
which condemns the unwarranted acquisition of undocumented personal
knowledge. . . . All of these [constitutional privacy] cases conflate the
right to privacy with the right to liberty.[38]

We can readily concur with Parent that an adequate account of
privacy should not confuse it with other related concepts such as
liberty or autonomy. And of course his concept of liberty is distinguishable from privacy as he has described it. But it is not at
all clear that Parent has shown that the constitutional privacy cases
involve no "genuine" privacy interests. His argument is not new,[39]
yet it has often been accepted with little comment.

There is a practical reason why the Court avoided using liberty
as the defense in the *Griswold* line of cases, although it does not
provide a rationale for why privacy was used. According to the
Fourteenth Amendment, no state shall deprive any person of life,
liberty, or property without due process of law. It was that "liberty" which was most commonly cited in a sequence of cases in
the early 1900s striking down nearly two hundred economic regulations, such as those fixing minimum wages for women.[40] But
the Court was not in those cases merely addressing fair procedures, and critics (led by Justice Oliver Wendell Holmes) felt that
the due process clause was being used in a substantive way to
scrutinize economic regulation carefully and to hold laws unconstitutional if the Court believed they were unwise. This substantive
due process doctrine, allowing courts to intrude on legislative
value judgments, was widely discredited and discarded by the late
1930s.[41]

Given the early association of a legal right to privacy as a right
to be let alone and the well-known explanation of a concept of
negative liberty in terms of freedom from interference, it is hardly
surprising that privacy and liberty should often be equated. But
our intuitive notion of privacy can be shown to be distinct from
liberty. For example, one's privacy may constantly be invaded by
surreptitious surveillance without affecting one's liberty, and
one's liberty may be invaded by assault, by conferring undesired

benefits, or by limiting one's choices (such as to burn the American flag)[42] without violating privacy interests. There are all sorts of liberties we do not have. I cannot leave the country without a passport; nor is George Carlin free to parody dirty words on the airwaves during daytime hours. But in neither case are we inclined to believe a privacy interest is at stake. As John Hart Ely has noted, "I suppose there is nothing to prevent one from using the word 'privacy' to mean the freedom to live one's life without governmental interference. But the Court obviously does not so use the term. Nor could it, for such a right is at stake in *every* case. Our lifestyles are constantly limited, often seriously, by governmental regulation."[43] Privacy may not always be well-protected either, but it is not understood by the Court or in our ordinary language to be as comprehensive an interest as freedom from governmental regulation.

Perhaps the relation between privacy and liberty in the *Griswold* line of cases can be understood as the constitutional right to privacy protecting certain liberties, namely the freedom to perform acts that do not affect the interests of others—what John Stuart Mill in *On Liberty* (1859) called "self-regarding" actions. With his juxtaposition of the terms, Mill himself gave the impression that both "liberty" and "privacy" characterize the realm of action he was most concerned to protect. He first described

a sphere of action in which society, as distinguished from the individual, has, if any, only an indirect interest: comprehending all that portion of a person's life and conduct which affects only himself, or, if it also affects others, only with their free, voluntary, and undeceived consent and participation. When I say only himself, I mean directly and in the first instance; for whatever affects himself may affect others through himself. . . . This, then, is the appropriate region of human *liberty*.[44] (my emphasis)

Yet only two paragraphs later, while defending the necessity of maintaining such liberty, he cautioned that while modern states have prevented great "interference by law in the details of *private* life," traditional tendencies have been just the opposite. "The ancient Commonwealths thought themselves entitled to practise, and the ancient philosophers countenanced, the regulation of every part of *private* conduct by public authority"[45] (my emphases).

However, in *Paris Adult Theatre* the Court clearly and effectively rejects the idea that constitutional privacy is merely freedom with respect to self-regarding acts.[46] It says, first, that the Constitution does not incorporate the proposition that conduct involving consenting adults is always beyond regulation, whereas the Constitution does provide a right of privacy. Hence the latter is not just a Mill-like right to freedom from legislative or other governmental interference in behavior that does not harm nonconsenting others. Second, the Court lays out the sorts of things that constitutional privacy does protect. Some of the activities protected, such as child-rearing, do not fall under a Mill-like right. And it appears from the Court's reasoning that some things covered by a Mill-like right—eating what one pleases, for example, or watching obscene movies in a public cinema in *Paris*—are not protected by the privacy right. Thus the constitutional right to privacy as it has developed is not even coextensional with Mill's right to freedom from governmental interference in behavior that does not prejudicially affect the welfare of others.

The constitutional privacy cases generally involve an interest in independence in making certain fundamental or personal decisions, and thus they do concern autonomy to determine for oneself what to do.[47] But because privacy does *not* just consist in possession of undocumented personal knowledge as Parent argued, and because an intuitive notion of privacy invoked in the constitutional privacy cases does *not* conflate privacy with autonomy and liberty as Henkin and Parent believe, we need not deny that there is a sense of privacy relevant to those cases. To the contrary, I have argued that it is more intuitive to agree that liberty, privacy, and autonomy are distinct concepts that overlap in their extensions. A subset of autonomy cases, including certain personal decisions regarding one's basic lifestyle that help define one's self-identity, can plausibly be said to involve privacy interests as well.

The view that no privacy interests are at stake in the constitutional cases is unhelpful at best and question-begging at worst. If one accepts a narrow definition of privacy such as Parent's concealment of information or Henkin's "hard-core" privacy, identifiable with traditional tort and Fourth Amendment protection, then the conclusion that privacy is irrelevant to the constitutional cases since *Griswold* follows trivially. But we have seen that while there are general intuitive differences between the tort and Fourth Amendment and the other constitutional privacy cases, it is more difficult to distinguish these than Henkin and others have allowed. Moreover, attempts to differentiate the two sorts of privacy claims reveal interesting ways in which they are related and highlight a more plausible explanation of the ways privacy and liberty are differentiable yet connected. Thus we can conclude that it will be more productive to understand privacy more broadly, as relevant to a wide range of cases where it has been claimed to be crucial.

THREE

Definitions of Privacy, Philosophical Responses, and Conceptual Alternatives

In this chapter I focus on philosophical responses to the legal debate about the scope of privacy. My goal is to sort out major definitional and conceptual questions about the meaning of privacy in light of the discussion of cases in preceding chapters. As we shall see, it is possible to fashion an inclusive account of privacy that allows us to explain both the existence of justifiable invasions of privacy and how protection of privacy preserves liberty.

Given the wide variety of privacy interests protected by law, it is not surprising that some commentators have suggested "privacy as but a name for a grab-bag of unrelated goodies."[1] As noted in chapter 2, Judith Thomson suggests that the right to privacy is not an independent right but is "derivative" from other rights, including property rights and rights to bodily security. According to this hypothesis, there is no such thing as *the* right to privacy, for any violation of a right to privacy violates some right not identical with or included in the right to privacy. Privacy is derivative in the sense that it is possible to explain each right in the cluster of privacy rights without ever mentioning the right to privacy.

Hence there is no need to find a particular commonality in the rights in the privacy cluster.

But as Thomas Scanlon, Jeffrey Reiman, William Parent, and other philosophers have persuasively countered, it is just as plausible that the reverse is true and that other rights such as those of ownership or liberty are "derivative" from privacy rights if there is something fundamental and of special value in privacy.[2] This view is reflected in public opinion surveys, which indicate that most Americans believe privacy in some sense is not only valuable but indeed crucial for a decent life. Attorney Janlori Goldman has noted:

> National polls document a growing demand for privacy protection. A *Trends and Forecasts* survey released in May, 1989 found that 7 out of 10 consumers feel that personal privacy is very important to them, with many expressing the fear that their privacy is in jeopardy.
>
> A June, 1990 survey by Louis Harris & Associates, *Consumers in the Information Age*, found a growing public demand for privacy legislation, documenting that an overwhelming majority of people believe that the right to privacy is in jeopardy. The survey also found that 79% of the American public stated that if the Declaration of Independence were rewritten today, they would add privacy to the list of "life, liberty and the pursuit of happiness" as a fundamental right.[3]

Unfortunately, nowhere is it articulated explicitly what Americans mean by "privacy" when they praise it in this way. Many scholars have attempted to give a definition of privacy or a characterization of privacy as a unitary concept. However, it is extremely difficult to isolate common elements in the diverse cases in which privacy is a crucial issue.

Philosophical Definitions of Privacy

As we saw in the last chapter, William Parent makes clear that he does not intend to identify privacy and secrecy. But if privacy is merely the condition of not having others possess certain information, apparently it *is* merely equivalent to *secrecy*. Nearly every dictionary includes a definition of privacy as secrecy or concealment. According to the *Oxford English Dictionary*, that which is private is "removed from public view or knowledge; not within the cognizance of people generally."[4] Private information is often that which is concealed, and interests in not being seen or overheard seem central to many privacy cases. But this merely shows that the concepts overlap. Privacy and secrecy are not coextensional. First, whatever is secret is withheld from others, and it may not always be private. Thus secret treaties or military plans kept from the public are not private transactions or information. Second, privacy does not always imply secrecy, for private information about one's debts or odd behavior may be publicized. Although it is no longer concealed, it is no less private.[5] Characterizing privacy as what is *intended* to be concealed is no help, as the above examples demonstrate. Military secrets are intended to be concealed; it does not follow that they are private. And information or intimate caresses may be private even if there is no intention to conceal them.[6]

Definitions of privacy also usually characterize privacy as *seclusion*, or the state or condition of being withdrawn from others, the observations of others, or the public interest.[7] Many of the cases Parent discusses as well as those arising in tort law seem to compel such an interpretation. Moreover, this definition may come closest to Judge Cooley's characterization of the right as "the right to be let alone." But even if a conversation or activity is private or very intimate, it will fail to be secluded if it is in public view or if it is overheard, seen, or otherwise observed by others. And discussion or activity intended to be private, such as child abuse or consenting sadomasochism, may be observed or may be of public concern. Conversely, even if a conversation or action is not in view of others, it may not be a private one in any sense except that it happens not to be observed or known about, even if it is of great public interest.

Some aspect of seclusion *is* clearly protected by privacy law. The American Law Institute's *Restatement of the Law of Torts*, (2d ed. 1976) includes a section titled "Intrusion on Seclusion" (§652B),

which reads: "One who intentionally intrudes, physically or otherwise, upon the solitude or seclusion of another, or his private
affairs or concerns, is subject to liability to the other for invasion
of his privacy, if the invasion would be highly offensive to a reasonable person." But this legal protection can be limited. What
would ordinarily be considered privacy interests are not always
protected if the individual involved is a public figure or if the
information is not confidential. A clandestine search (without a
warrant) through office files was not considered an invasion of
privacy, despite a loss of privacy, since the information gathered
and publicized was needed to judge the individual as a candidate
for the U.S. Senate.[8] And when Ralph Nader complained that
prior to his publication of *Unsafe at Any Speed*, General Motors
agents interviewed acquaintances about his political, racial, and
sexual views; kept him under surveillance in public places; attempted to entrap him with women; made threatening, harassing,
and obnoxious telephone calls to him; tapped his telephone; and
eavesdropped on private conversations by means of mechanical
and electronic equipment, the court asserted that "mere gathering of information about a particular individual does not give rise
to a cause of action under this theory. Privacy is invaded only if
the information sought is of a confidential nature and the defendant's conduct was unreasonably intrusive."[9]

According to the opinion in Nader's case, *confidential content* is
crucial to privacy. Yet other tort privacy claims are upheld because
of the intrusiveness of the behavior, even if the information or
photographs obtained are not at all confidential. For example, in
Dietemann v. Time Inc., two *Life* magazine reporters entered the
home of a disabled veteran under false pretenses and took clandestine photographs and recordings to learn about and publicize
the quackery being practiced there.[10] It was held and affirmed on
appeal that this was an invasion of privacy even though the content was not confidential; indeed, whether or not the material was
published was not relevant.

The courts are clearly puzzled over the relationship among privacy and seclusion, confidential content, publicity, and intrusiveness, perhaps because of their concern with the public interest.

Moreover, secrecy, seclusion, and confidential content alone fail to give an adequate philosophical account of the realm of the private, although each may be a crucial aspect of some subset of privacy invasions. Unfortunately, commentators in law and philosophy have rarely acknowledged or addressed this confusion. I suggest, however, that most who assess the cases find the *Nader* decision outrageous, think the *Dietemann* result reasonable, and believe the opera singer's privacy in Thomson's example (described in chapter 2) has been invaded. If so, this is further evidence that acquisition of undocumented personal knowledge is not always relevant to a privacy intrusion.[11] Our privacy interests are both more extensive and deeper than any of the definitions we have discussed allows. Thus there is good reason to believe that we can offer neither a simple, unique definition of privacy nor an analysis of the concept in terms of necessary and sufficient conditions.

Conceptual Alternatives

Suppose we agree to reject the view that privacy has narrow scope and consequently is irrelevant to the constitutional cases. We then have at least the following two options: (i) We might further emphasize and draw out similarities between tort and constitutional privacy claims in order to develop a notion of privacy fundamental to informational and Fourth Amendment privacy concerns as well as to the *Griswold* line of constitutional cases. This seems to be a promising approach. Consider consenting sexual intimacy between persons of the same sex in a shared home or the home of one of the partners, for instance. Regardless of one's assessment of the behavior, one may view it as a private matter, whether the state is seeking to *regulate the behavior* or if others are attempting to *gain or exploit information* about it.

(ii) We could concede that whatever "privacy" means in the tort and Fourth Amendment cases, it means something different in the constitutional cases. Nevertheless, we might take that "something else" seriously as a distinct but legitimate use of the term, which is not "spurious" but is reflected in our ordinary language. There are reasons to believe that (ii) may also be a fruitful alternative. After all, contrary to Henkin's view that tort privacy is "what most people mean by privacy," the term is often used in contexts beyond informational privacy that are clearly related to the interests at stake in the constitutional cases. For example, in a pamphlet explaining how to protect children by teaching them how to say "No!" to strangers without making them needlessly fearful or antisocial, parents and teachers are told, "Children have the right to privacy. Teach it. Reinforce it. One of the ways to help children prevent sexual assault is to encourage them to develop a sense of physical integrity. A sense that they have a right to their own body space and privacy. Just as we allow them to close the door when they use the bathroom, we must also allow them to say no to any unwanted physical affection and touch."[12] No doubt this extended usage has developed in part because of the Supreme Court's use of the term "privacy" in the constitutional cases since 1965, but whatever the reason, a broad use of the term is now common in our language.

Unfortunately, the most obvious starting point for identifying the sense of privacy that is relevant to the constitutional cases is extremely worrisome. In *Roe v. Wade*, the Court itself has said, "Only personal rights that can be deemed 'fundamental' . . . are included in this guarantee of personal privacy. . . . [T]he right has some extension to activities relating to marriage[,] . . . procreation[,] . . . contraception[,] . . . family relationships[,] . . . and child rearing and education."[13] The difficulty, of course, is that little more is offered by way of explaining which rights are "personal" or "fundamental" or both. Focusing on marriage makes *Roe* difficult to understand, given that Jane Roe was unmarried, and attending only to family issues does not help us make sense of the *Stanley* case, which protects one's right to view pornography in one's home. It is also problematic that decisions such as what color shoes to wear are reasonably viewed as personal yet are far from fundamental enough to warrant special protection. Moreover, regulations such as those governing the draft or employment are not usually viewed as privacy invasions, although they might be said to interfere with matters of one's life that are both fundamental and personal in the vague sense described by the Court.

It is worth noting, however, that even in tort law the notion of privacy has been evolving through a constellation of judgments. Although there is no fixed way of using the term that we can then proceed to analyze, the concept of privacy has not in those cases been taken to be meaningless or empty. To take a related example, the term "freedom" has varied meanings. Although there is no unitary and single definition of freedom, the term is nevertheless useful and meaningful in many contexts. It may be, then, that there is reason to believe that the scope of a "personal and fundamental" notion of privacy relevant to the constitutional cases can be further delineated through a consideration of cases, especially since it seems to me that in many cases application of the term is clear and unproblematic. A decision to have a vasectomy, for example, can uncontroversially be said to be a personal and fundamental one, and it is in that sense private. Suppose we deny that this important sense of privacy is relevant to that decision merely because autonomy to determine for oneself what one ought to do is also at risk. We then fail to acknowledge the personal significance in an individual's life of forcing on him or refusing him the operation.

The problem remains, however, of somehow clarifying the meaning and scope of privacy as that "something else" relevant in the constitutional cases. Moreover, once it is settled that something is a private matter, it is a separate issue to decide whether or not, in some social context, an invasion of it can be justified. I believe, for example, that a mandatory sterilization program for male recidivists or for those in a country suffering grave poverty and overpopulation *does* invade privacy, and the social or legal question is whether or not the invasion can, in particular circumstances, be justified. Although all will agree that both individual and social interests must be balanced by moral philosophers as well as the courts, we will not always agree on the weight to be accorded individual claims.

Let us return, then, to alternative (i), according to which we draw on similarities between tort and constitutional privacy claims in order to develop a notion of privacy fundamental to informational and Fourth Amendment privacy concerns as well as to the other constitutional cases. One reason neither Parent's definition nor secrecy, seclusion, or confidential content alone is helpful for an adequate characterization of privacy is that they lead us to focus on what is *as a matter of fact* hidden or confidential.

In an effort to distinguish the descriptive sense of "privacy" from a normative use that encompasses interests *worthy* of protection (some subset of which, depending on the circumstances, actually are protected), some commentators have suggested that privacy must be not merely the absence of others who have information but individual *control* over knowledge that others have about one. While the interest was first discussed as control over *information* others have about oneself, it has been extended to include control over *actions* as well, that is, what one does or has done to one. On this view, advocated by Ernst van den Haag, for example, and defended in a somewhat altered form by Ruth Gavison, privacy is a power to deny or grant access.[14]

But surely not every loss or gain of control over information about us or what we do or have done to us is a loss or gain of privacy. For example, a writer's research may inadvertently display her shabby or inaccurate scholarship. Alternatively, as Richard Parker suggests,

Consider the student whose examination unexpectedly reveals that he has not studied, or imagine the person who is snubbed at a party by the guest of honor, revealing to all present his low standing with that guest. In both cases, and in others like them, information about these people becomes known to others without their consent. They lose control of it; yet we would not say that they have suffered a loss of privacy.[15]

Similarly, if a police officer pushes one out of the way of an ambulance, one has lost control of what is done to one, but we would not say that privacy has been invaded. Not just any touching is a privacy intrusion. It is thus much too broad to characterize a privacy interest as an ability to control.

Nevertheless, it may be that loss of control over some aspect of

oneself is a *necessary* condition for a loss of privacy. Perhaps for
every privacy intrusion the individual loses control over what is
seen, heard, or read about him, over what is done with information, recordings, or photographs of her, over what is done to him
(e.g., he is wired or operated on without consent), or over what
she does (e.g., chooses to use contraceptives or read pornography). On this view privacy and control are closely linked. If this
is so, then we might extend a traditional notion of property to
include whatever one has control over. On this account every privacy invasion would also be a property invasion, but not the reverse, so that privacy interests would form a subset of property
interests. We would be claiming that not only our bodies, minds,
and written work but also our reputations, information about us,
and so on are our property, thus stretching considerably our common notion of property. Then any right to privacy is a right to
exclude others from some property. This is apparently van den
Haag's view. "Privacy is best treated as a property right," he states,
and he focuses on exclusivity as the core of privacy when he defines privacy as exclusive access of a person to a realm of his own.[16]

I am concerned, however, that our intuitive sense of property
rights breaks down in privacy contexts. Do we "own" behavior we
do not want observed, or all the information we want or have a
right to suppress? It is doubtful as well that we own our bodies in
as straightforward and uncomplicated a sense as we own letters
or land. We certainly do not own the thoughts in others' minds
or their attitudes. It is more worrisome that even if van den Haag's
thesis could be defended adequately, focus on control or property
ownership may not offer a *full explanation* of privacy issues. It may
fail to capture what is distinctive and most fundamental in the
diverse privacy cases. Others seem to agree that privacy cannot be
explained adequately in terms of control. Jeffrey Reiman writes,
"Privacy must be a condition independent of the issue of control.
. . . The right to privacy is not my right to control access to me—it
is my right that others be deprived of that access. In some cases,
though not all, having this right will protect my ability to control
access to me."[17]

Noting that mention of "personal" rights is prominent in the

Court's explanation of constitutional privacy, one might think that whether a privacy invasion involves information about oneself, bodily security, or choices about one's lifestyle, it always intrudes on a special zone close to oneself, something very *personal.* According to the *Oxford English Dictionary,* what is private affects "a person, or a small intimate body or group of persons apart from the general community; [it is] individual, personal."[18] One feature of Parent's definition that we did not reject in the last chapter was his focus on "personal" information. While he characterizes only information as personal, we might attempt to extend the characterization to cover activities as well as information, in order to generate a broader notion of privacy. But recall that for Parent what is personal is relativized to individuals, and it includes not only what most would choose not to share but also what a particular individual is "acutely sensitive" about. There are of course well-known difficulties with legal protection of peculiar sensitivities, and we might do better to adopt a "reasonable person" standard of what is personal. Yet problems with this focus on the personal still remain. If you tap my phone but merely hear me placing an order for pizza, it seems reasonable to agree that you violated my privacy although you heard no personal information and had no physical access to me. And a decision to merge one's business with another's may be a private but not a personal matter. Such cases indicate that concentrating on what is personal either will be vacuous or will not adequately circumscribe what we understand as the scope of privacy.

Similar problems confront accounts of privacy expressed in terms of the requirements for friendship or intimacy. Consider, for example, the approach taken by Julie Inness in her recent book, *Privacy, Intimacy, and Isolation.*[19] She too defends privacy as having broad scope, encompassing both tort and constitutional privacy claims, and she identifies *intimacy* as the defining feature of those invasions properly termed "privacy invasions." According to Inness, intimacy is based not on behavior but on motivation, so intimate information or activity is that which draws its meaning from an agent's love, liking, or care. Constitutional privacy cases, on this view, do concern autonomous decision making, and they are "genuine" privacy cases when the decision is an intimate one. Thus the constitutional privacy cases form a subset of autonomy cases, and the notions of privacy and autonomy as the freedom to choose are differentiable, though connected. Despite her intentions to the contrary, an account such as Inness's does not completely explain the full range of privacy concerns in tort and constitutional law. Information about one's salary and credit records, for example, is information people often choose to keep private and desire to have protected, but it is difficult to see how to categorize such information as intimate.

We do, however, have a crude intuition that what is private is that which is "nobody else's business." This is reminiscent of Joel Feinberg's suggestion that "it may be stretching things a bit to use one label, 'the right to privacy,' for such a diversity of rights, except to indicate that there is a realm (or a number of realms) of human conduct that are simply nobody's business except that of the actors, and a fortiori are beyond the legitimate attention of the criminal law."[20] In view of this, we might take the realm of the private to be whatever is not the legitimate concern of others: those others may be private individuals in tort cases, the government for constitutional claims.

Despite the vagueness of this characterization, we can agree that information as well as activities and decisions can be private in this sense, allowing a basic conceptual relationship between tort and constitutional privacy interests. On this account privacy will have a normative component, and privacy claims may be made by individuals, couples, or small groups. Because some trivial claims may on this interpretation be private, there will be a broad spectrum of more and less important privacy interests. Moreover, what is legitimately the concern of others can vary according to circumstances and culture. Thus we might agree that in this country, a couple's decision about whether or not to use contraceptives is beyond the legitimate concern of others, whereas it is at least arguable that governmental intrusion in such a decision could be legitimate in overpopulated countries such as China or India.

The first and most obvious worry is that this account is overbroad. Consider, for example, John Locke's principle that religious ends are not a legitimate state concern.[21] If we wish to distinguish privacy from religious claims, among others, we must seek an explanation of which subclass of issues beyond the legitimate concern of others constitute the private interests. I address this issue in the next chapter.

Second, if characterization of the private as that which is not the legitimate concern of others is to be useful, the notion of "legitimacy" needs closer scrutiny. Many cases will be clear. For example, neither my bathroom behavior nor information about it can be justified as the legitimate concern of others, given that I have no communicable diseases or tendencies dangerous to myself or others. In contrast, there is wide disagreement over whether or not a decision to have an abortion is a proper concern of others beyond the mother. And even if we believe that details about one's sex life are not the kind of information that is the legitimate concern of the state, we might have great difficulty determining whether or not, for an individual with AIDS, the danger of the disease and our knowledge about its transmission justify viewing detailed information about that individual's sex life as legitimately of public concern. In later chapters I consider particular cases in order to demonstrate ways to balance privacy against other interests and claims.

Unfortunately there is a third, more serious difficulty with this proposal.[22] As presented, it does not allow us to account for the existence of *justifiable* invasions of privacy. If, for example, we determine that when an individual has AIDS, details about his sex life are legitimately the concern of state health officials wishing to compile the accurate information on incidence and transmission of the disease essential for an effective public health response, then according to the explanation given we must agree that there is no privacy invasion when officials inquire about those intimacies. But this seems incorrect. What we want to say in such a case is that seeking such information *is* an invasion of the privacy of the person with AIDS, but that the intrusion is justified because of the seriousness of the health threat from a fatal and communicable condition.

Perhaps the best way to handle this difficulty is to characterize the realm of the private as whatever is not generally—that is, according to a reasonable person under normal circumstances, or according to certain social conventions—a legitimate concern of others. Privacy will thus be a property of *types* of information and activities, and we may say that any interference with them will be a privacy invasion, although particular interferences can be justified. This general explanation can then be filled out more fully by supplying more details about determining which circumstances and conventions are relevant and by describing types of acts for particular cases.

This sort of account does have the advantage of allowing us to clarify an important relationship between privacy and liberty. As we have seen, loss of privacy can diminish freedom. Nevertheless, defending privacy cannot always protect liberty. It cannot guard against public assault, for example. But if privacy protects against certain intrusions by others, and if one has liberty when one is free of external restraints and interferences, then protection of privacy can preserve some liberty. We can in this way make sense of Parent's claim "that privacy is a moral value for persons who also prize freedom and individuality."[23]

A further benefit of this approach is worth noting. Parent and Richard Posner have objected that currently informational privacy is less well protected than the constitutional right to privacy. If a reasonable person would not be troubled by publicity about a family wedding of the sort Warren and Brandeis reportedly sought to obviate, then in such cases privacy may well be a petty tort.[24] And if in the balance it is more important to exclude the state from decisions about whether or not to have a vasectomy, or to acquire contraceptive information and devices, than to have security against embarrassment arising from the use of one's name, correspondence, or photograph, then we may be able to support this recent trend over Parent's and Posner's complaints against it.[25]

Some words of caution are in order, however. The "reasonable person" standard is familiar in a variety of contexts in the law. Yet we may well wonder whether there really is a unitary, objective, and universal reasonable person standard that can be described and applied, or whether such a standard is deeply problematic. We need to inquire, in particular, the extent to which the concept imbeds norms that do not fit members of nondominant groups who have grown up under "irregular" circumstances—in economic deprivation, for instance. Different backgrounds are likely to lead people to have vastly different ideas concerning what counts as worthy of protection as a matter of privacy. Hence it may be, as Kim Lane Scheppele suggests, that "women, people of color, and other politically disadvantaged groups are ill-served by a standardized concept of a reasonable man or an average person or a point-of-viewless point of view."[26]

This is an important concern for the broad conceptual account of privacy proposed thus far, but it is not an insurmountable one. The law is already evolving to recognize a multiplicity of reasonable points of view in other contexts, as Scheppele observes:

In a number of areas of the law, courts already find ways to incorporate the distinctive social knowledge of socially diverse actors. In tort cases, for example, courts adopt some formulation, either explicitly or implicitly, that inquires into what the reasonable man would have done under the circumstances. As tort doctrine has evolved, the unitary reasonable man has multiplied into the reasonably prudent doctor, the reasonable pilot, and the ordinarily careful horse trainer, among other characters recognizable in law. This multiplication of types of persons shows that existing legal doctrine and considerations of fairness do not require that everyone's perceptions be measured against the same social standard of reasonableness. But the law only incompletely recognizes that special knowledge is acquired not only in occupations but also in other sociological categories that give rise to different ways of seeing the world. . . . Being female or a person of color in this society is relevant to one's social point of view, and the law would better serve everyone if it recognized that the melting pot no longer melts all points of view into one, if indeed it ever did.[27]

Scheppele expands on this theme to argue for a "reasonable woman" standard, with gender-specific content, especially for determining consent in rape cases. She points out that such a stan-

dard is not new, although it is still controversial. Thus a number
of courts have said the point of view of a reasonable woman
should be adopted to determine whether men's behavior in the
workplace is disruptive enough to qualify as sexual harassment.[28]
The standard has appeared as well in murder cases in which a
woman has killed her batterer.

In adapting a reasonable person standard to privacy cases,
courts must assess the threat to privacy from the point of view of
those in need of protection. The idea is not to grant some higher
level of protection but to incorporate the experiences of others
and their perceptions of the world, in a good faith attempt to
understand that people differently situated in the social order
may *reasonably* assess levels of intrusiveness and their own vulnerability differently. Consequently we need not reject the reasonable
person standard. Nevertheless, courts will need to continue the
process begun in other types of cases which use a standard of
reasonableness that accounts for sensitivity to the viewpoints of
other groups.[29]

This is an alternative approach to privacy, a broad conception
encompassing both tort and constitutional privacy claims, where
privacy is a property of types of information and activity viewed
by a reasonable person in normal circumstances as beyond the
legitimate concern of others. Such an account allows us to explain
the existence of justifiable invasions of privacy and the relationship between privacy and liberty. But to be illuminating it must
be narrowed to explain which subset of interests not legitimately
the concern of others are best understood as privacy interests.

Defending a Broad Conception of Privacy

We have seen that it is not possible to give a unique, unitary definition of privacy that covers all the diverse privacy interests. The other extreme—abandoning the notion of privacy as meaningless or completely derivative from other interests such as property or bodily security—is equally untenable. My approach, therefore, is to take a middle course. In this chapter I defend privacy as a broad and multifaceted cluster concept, mark out the contexts where it is natural to view privacy as crucial, and propose a strategy for balancing privacy against competing claims and values.

Similarities between Diverse Privacy Interests

Clearly there is some intuitive difference between the privacy interests described by the Supreme Court as (i) an "individual interest in avoiding disclosure of personal matters" and (ii) an "interest in independence in making certain kinds of important decisions."[1] But I wish to demonstrate that the similarity of reasons given for protection of privacy in varied cases provides a philosophically sound justification for relating tort, Fourth Amendment, and other constitutional privacy claims. Moreover, it is historically accurate to relate this broad range of privacy interests. There is thus a strong positive argument for characterizing and defending privacy as a broad and inclusive concept, important in a wide range of cases that protect our ability to control information about ourselves, our ability to govern access to ourselves, and our ability to make self-expressive autonomous decisions free from intrusion or control by others.

A somewhat different argument for the conclusion that privacy embraces these varied interests has been given by Laurence Tribe.

Whatever the outcome of the philosophical debate between those who regard privacy as but a name for a grab-bag of unrelated goodies and those who think it a unitary concept,[2] these kinds of definitional attempts share two important limitations. First, however helpful taxonomies might be, they usually leave unspecified the substance of what is being protected, telling us neither the character of the choices or information we are to classify as special, nor the contexts of decision in which such classification is to be employed. . . . Second, by focusing on the inward-looking face of privacy, the taxonomies slight those equally central outward-looking aspects of self that are expressed less through demanding secrecy, sanctuary, or seclusion than through seeking to project one identity rather than another upon the public world. . . . [T]his outward-looking dimension of personality . . . seem[s] artificially severed from the more introspective side of the "right to be let alone" in the categorizations attempted to date.[3]

As Tribe is quick to note, however, "the urge to confine 'privacy' to the inward dimension is certainly understandable. A concept in danger of embracing everything is a concept in danger of embracing nothing."[4]

In the previous chapter I developed a proposal that takes the realm of the private to be whatever is not, according to a reasonable person in normal circumstances, the legitimate concern of others. Clearly, the proposal as it stands is vague and overbroad. We might then worry that this proposal or any other comprehensive characterization of privacy may be too general to be very useful, especially since privacy violations can be so varied: they can arise from misuse of confidential information, from conduct that is intrusive even if no information is gained or disclosed, from disturbance of an intimate relationship, or from disruption of various other important aspects of one's life. But I believe this proposal can be supplemented so that it is both useful and illuminating. Ronald Dworkin has observed of another concept, "Equality is a popular but mysterious political ideal. People can become equal (or at least more equal) in one way with the consequence that they become unequal (or more unequal) in others. . . . It does not follow that equality is worthless as an ideal."[5] So too with privacy: the concept may be popular, mysterious, and elusive, and there may be different types of privacy or ways in which one can gain or lose privacy. It does not follow that privacy is either worthless or too vague to be meaningful as an ideal.

Even if privacy claims are many and diverse, and do not derive from any single, overarching right to privacy, they may yet have a common foundation in basic conceptual similarities between tort, Fourth Amendment, and other constitutional privacy interests. Tribe has alluded to this conceptual relationship by noting, "Of concern . . . is any system of governmental information-gathering, information-preservation, and/or information-dissemination that threatens to leave individuals with insufficient control over who knows what about their lives. Such control must be understood as a basic part of the right to shape the 'self' that one presents to the world, and on the basis of which the world in turn shapes one's existence."[6] I believe it is possible to develop an even more specific way of identifying the similarities between informational privacy and privacy surrounding bodily integrity and self-identity: namely, by demonstrating that people seek privacy protection for tort and Fourth Amendment as well as varied constitutional privacy concerns because of a range of similar reasons.

People have many different reasons for wanting to control information about themselves, motives ranging from freedom from defamation to commercial gain. When freedom from scrutiny, embarrassment, judgment, and even ridicule are at stake, as well as protection from pressure to conform, prejudice, emotional distress, and the losses in self-esteem, opportunities, or finances arising from these harms, we are more inclined to view the claim to control information as a privacy claim. A tort privacy action and Fourth Amendment claim are two mechanisms society has created to accomplish such protection. By themselves they are not wholly adequate, however, because the interests that justify the screen on information include the interest in being free to decide absent the threat of the same problems that accompany an information leak. In other words, it is plausible to maintain that worries about what information others have are often *due* to worries about social control. What you can do to me, or what I can do free of the threat of scrutiny, judgment, and so on, may often depend on what information (personal or not) you, the state, or others have about me. Since my behavior is also affected by the extent to which I can make my own choices, both the threat of an information leak and the threat of decreased control over decision making can have a chilling effect on my behavior.

Thus the desire to protect a sanctuary for ourselves, a refuge within which we can shape and carry on our lives and relationships with others—intimacies as well as other activities—without the threat of scrutiny, embarrassment, judgment, and the deleterious consequences they might bring, is a major underlying reason for providing *both* information control and control over decision making. Furthermore, since people want control over many things, and freedom is far broader than privacy, this similarity of reasons for protecting tort and constitutional privacy interests is more fundamental than the idea that both involve freedom or control.

While we still have no unified definition of privacy, this examination of reasons for protecting privacy does indicate that privacy claims can be identified by looking at the justifications for such claims. Consequently, we can say that an interest in privacy is at stake when intrusion by others is not legitimate *because* it jeopardizes or prohibits protection of a realm free from scrutiny, judgment, and the pressure, distress, or losses they can cause. While this list of reasons for protecting privacy is not exhaustive, it clearly shows a range of similar reasons for guarding tort privacy protection over information, Fourth Amendment privacy protection over access, and constitutional privacy protection over decision making and self-expressive behavior, reasons that can be used to demarcate those intrusions reasonably viewed as privacy invasions. Moreover, their similarity offers persuasive evidence that these interests are related in a philosophically important way and that a meaningful interest in privacy is at stake in a wide range of tort, Fourth Amendment, and other constitutional privacy cases.

I argued in chapter 2 that in tort and Fourth Amendment law as well as constitutional law, privacy protects both peace of mind and bodily integrity. There is evidence, moreover, that it is historically accurate to relate tort, Fourth Amendment, and constitutional privacy claims. As noted in chapter 1, a multiplicity of arguments from the first tort privacy case, *Pavesich*, reemerged in the foundational constitutional privacy case, *Griswold v. Connecticut.* Prior to *Pavesich*, Judge Cooley's characterization of the right to privacy as the "right to be let alone" was used by Warren and Brandeis as a starting point for their argument, which favored tort law protection for emotional harms generated by publication or appropriation not relevant to the public interest. Even commentators antagonistic to the constitutional right of privacy acknowledge that in his treatise on torts Cooley indicated he had a much broader right in mind, including personal security and bodily integrity.[7] Moreover, in 1891 Cooley's right was cited in justifying a privacy interest that is far closer to interests currently protected in constitutional cases than those Warren and Brandeis argued for in tort law. In *Union Pacific Railway v. Botsford*, Clara Botsford was not required to submit to a surgical examination by her adversary as to the extent of the injury sued for. Justice Gray delivered the opinion of the Court:

No right is held more sacred, or is more carefully guarded by common law, than the right of every individual to the possession and control of his own person, free from all restraint or interference of others. . . . As well said by *Judge* Cooley, "The right to one's person may be said to be a right of complete immunity: to be let alone. . . ." The inviolability of the person is as much invaded by a compulsory stripping or exposure as by a blow.[8]

Recall, too, that the use of the term "privacy" in the wide range of cases cited is familiar in our ordinary linguistic usage in political, religious, biological, anthropological, and sociological contexts.

This discussion demonstrates that the close relationship between tort, Fourth Amendment, and constitutional privacy claims is philosophically well-motivated, historically accurate, and reflected in ordinary language—all considerations that justify a broad conception of privacy. It is plausible to believe that this means privacy is essential for one's self-esteem and sense of identity, providing the ability to maintain presumptive control and decision-making power not only over what information others have about oneself and for what purpose, but also over who has access to oneself and what personal activities and relationships one can pursue without intrusion by others. We can thus view privacy interests as those beyond the legitimate concern of others *for a certain set of reasons*, such as freedom from scrutiny, judgment, and pressure to conform or to reveal one's weaknesses and vulnerabilities. On this view our privacy interests derive from a need for independence that is broader than narrow theories of privacy based on information, autonomy, property, or intimacy allow.

It is important, however, to circumscribe the realm of privacy encompassing this wide array of interests by describing the *types* of information and activity that a reasonable person would normally consider illegitimate arenas for interference by others *because of* the threat of scrutiny, embarrassment, ridicule, or coercion such an intrusion would allow. One of the difficulties, of course, is that private realms are distinguished in a variety of contexts, including domestic life, markets and political economy, and the legal enforcement of morality. Thus I believe it is most useful to identify aspects of privacy, perhaps overlapping, that protect clusters of privacy interests. The development of privacy law to date helps us begin the process. But it is also productive to view concern for privacy protection as evolving from the sort of values inherent in historical discussions of privacy and other constitutional guarantees, values expressed in vague language whose interpretation new technology and situations make more pressing and difficult.

Recent work on privacy by Ferdinand David Schoeman is particularly insightful and useful in supplementing current explanations of privacy. Schoeman elicits numerous values underlying privacy protection by considering our nature as persons, what moves us to desire or require privacy, and what we lose without it. Our maintenance of self-respect requires privacy, and control over some sphere of our lives and information about us is essential if we are to be independent human beings able to grow, strive, and accomplish, free from the pressure, emotional stress, prejudice, or loss of self-esteem and opportunities that can accompany privacy deprivation.

Schoeman on the Social Dimension of Privacy

In his 1992 book, *Privacy and Social Freedom*, Ferdinand Schoeman defends a broad characterization of privacy and examines its role in social contexts that can help us better understand the meaning and scope of privacy. His declared aim is to understand the dimensions of privacy that arise in our social encounters, not merely privacy claims made against governments. It is his view that previous work on privacy has "omitted an especially important dimension of privacy: the form and function of privacy in promoting social freedom,"[9] or privacy as an indispensable tool that protects people in ordinary social contexts. Schoeman goes on to explain some provocative implications of his views for the analysis of human nature in social psychology and for an understanding of moral theory that integrates our experience as socially dependent beings. My focus, however, is his discussion of privacy.

Schoeman first argues that despite the almost irresistible inclination to try to define a concept like privacy as a means of addressing the controversy surrounding it, there may actually be some benefit in not embracing a definition too eagerly or hastily. On his view, "we can better understand privacy by characterizing the contexts in which it arises or is invoked as a concern" (11). Recognizing that privacy clearly represents different things to different people, and is valued differently as well, Schoeman introduces a novel distinction between two types of privacy norms. (i) Some social norms restrict access of others to an individual in a domain where the individual is granted wide discretion concerning how to behave in that domain. This sort of restricted access privacy promotes individuality, associations with others, and the ability to carve out a personal lifestyle. (ii) But there are also social norms that can restrict access to an individual in a domain where the behavior carried on in "private" is already rigidly defined by social norms allowing little discretion—for example, norms surrounding excretion and bathroom behavior. The point of such norms is not the enhancement of individual choice or expression. Rather, the privacy accorded here "manifests a rigid and internalized form of social control" (15), indeed enhancing control, not liberation. While Schoeman does not use this description, perhaps we could think of such norms as providing comfort, sanctuary, and freedom from scrutiny in cases where we tend to be somewhat sensitive and uncomfortable, perhaps precisely because of the restrictive social norms and taboos already in existence.

According to Schoeman, while both sorts of norms are privacy norms that "typically relate to our practices of showing respect for people and are reflections of social structure and symbolism" (16), and both restrict others' access to an individual, their functions are otherwise distinct. The latter type of social norms can function to protect human dignity "by protecting us from public association with the beastly, the unclean" (17), whereas privacy norms of the former type free people from social control and thus provide a way of respecting an additional component of human dignity that emerges in various cultural settings. He suggests that the controlling privacy norms can evolve into liberating ones. Schoeman argues that failing to draw this distinction between privacy norms has impeded our understanding of major cultural dimensions of privacy. I think we would do well to understand why.

Privacy that restricts others' access in areas already highly regulated evolves from what Schoeman calls *functional* roles and can reflect social taboos. In contrast, privacy that restricts access to allow for individual self-expression arises from *expressive* roles. These latter roles, according to Schoeman, "involve an individual distinctively and personally" and "are ones in which an individual is most exposed and vulnerable" (18). Expression and personal development of this sort, which allow for exploration, presuppose trust and vulnerability, and hence they cannot flourish without the type of privacy that promotes self-expression. Indeed, our emotional vulnerability, which makes us fit subjects of moral caring, is a basis for expressive privacy. Privacy protects us from exposure where we are vulnerable in that way. Schoeman's focus is on this latter, expressive-role privacy protection, and his recognition of the importance of privacy norms that enable and enhance personal expression and the development of relationships is both novel and important. Furthermore, it confirms the conceptual relationships I have defended and legitimizes my interpretation of the scope of privacy as broader and more inclusive than in accounts focusing on mere informational privacy or restrictions of physical access. Other activities and personal choices will be peculiarly self-expressive and hence will fall within the domain of privacy.

Schoeman's view helps make possible a fuller understanding of why autonomy and privacy may both be at stake in the constitutional privacy cases although these are still "genuine" privacy cases. Autonomy is required for people to be self-expressive. But the point of such autonomy, understood as successful control over one's life and values, is not to disengage one from relations but to enhance one's ability to form new and deeper relationships. In addition, privacy and autonomy are related because both suggest that others have no business crossing a threshold.

Privacy is important and has value, then, "largely because of how it facilitates associations and relational ties with others, not independence from people" (8). The restrictions on access that privacy protects do not just isolate people but enable them to form associations that serve their personal and group goals. Thus privacy not merely *excludes* (e.g., business or government or others), as van den Haag argued, but also protects the ability to form meaningful relationships. In this sense it has a central social dimension and a role in regulating important domains of social interaction. The way privacy functions in social contexts is what has been too often missed, perhaps because of moral theory's focus on rationality as well as on public and generally applicable standards. Schoeman does not deny that privacy is critical to individual creativity, but he wants to call attention to the relational dimensions of privacy that have often been ignored or underemphasized.

In sum, we have a rich, new explanation of privacy's role and value. In Schoeman's words, "privacy norms serve the same function vis-à-vis social coercion that constitutional principles serve vis-à-vis legal coercion, protecting individuals from the overreaching control of others. Of course, not all constitutional principles protect people from the powerful and not all privacy principles shield people from social pressures. But some do, and when they do, they restrain and channel power" (22–23). When privacy norms are effective in this way, they protect potentialities and vulnerabilities, which can change with historical and cultural circumstances. Privacy then shields people from inappropriate manifestations of social pressure that can preclude individual self-expression as well as deeper and more variable associations with others. This account is a functional and relativistic account, engaging variable norms of privacy to enable individuals to develop in ways not subject to overreaching social pressures. There is no intrinsically rightful domain of the private. Rather, "because what counts as expressing the individual's self and what counts as overreaching interference with this self vary with context and domain, . . . what privacy legitimately protects will vary" (113). In addition, expressive-role privacy most likely evolves, in Schoeman's view, only in societies that are materially secure and liberated from dependence on any group, societies in which welfare and security depend on individual initiative.

What, then, are the relations between privacy, freedom, and control that emerge from this approach? Privacy functions not just as a right but as a system of social norms mitigating the effectiveness of other systems of control over an individual. It protects individuals from the overreaching social control of others, thus serving as a counterbalance. But it is itself then a part of social control strategies, as it enables individuals and groups the space to create their own norms. Privacy limits access to others not merely in their "private" lives but in all domains of life, and it thus empowers individuals to control their self-expression and associations. It is "a means of regulating the amount of social control afforded individuals within associations, both public and private" (192; see also 22, 137, 142, 165). Privacy functions, then, to limit external and inappropriate social control, and to enhance internal control over self-expression and interpersonal relationships.

With respect to freedom, Schoeman focuses on one form of privacy that promotes, sustains, and facilitates social freedom. His notion of freedom from overreaching social control replaces John Stuart Mill's freedom from overreaching social influence. On Mill's view, one is socially free so long as one does not succumb to intimidation from social reproach and is not socially punished for self-regarding beliefs or attitudes or behavior, however unpopular they may be. For Mill, acting because of social pressure makes us less free, less rational, and less autonomous. For Schoeman, in contrast, "social freedom is grounded in availability of alternative systems of social support for individual and group projects" (98). Social freedom is enhanced by our associations with others and by the attendant social pressures, which help social groups maintain their structure, direction, and effectiveness. Thus we are free from the power of the state or society not when we act without reference to the attitudes of others, as Mill advocated, but when we have diverse social groups available to which we can adhere and contribute, and from which we can gain support. We exercise our freedom not by indifference to others but by belonging to and participating in various associations as we choose. In this way we express ourselves as effective agents of social change. We can therefore see how Schoeman has established, and helped make more salient, "the connecting, rather than the conflicting, features of the categories: freedom, control, agency, and privacy" (156–157).

It is interesting to note that while Schoeman occasionally mentions intimacy, and clearly believes intimate relationships are *one sort* of association that privacy protects, intimacy is no longer as central here as it was in some of his earlier work on privacy. What is "intimate," based on its root meaning, is that which is innermost for a person. Intimate activities will thus be those that expose one's vulnerability. But Schoeman leaves it open, correctly I believe, for privacy to protect more than what is intimate in this sense.

Nevertheless, his discussion raises some questions about the realm of the private at the same time that it answers others. For example, we might wonder what more can be said to clarify the notion of individual self-expression crucial to his explanation. Schoeman recognizes, as I have emphasized, that what counts as expressing the individual's self will vary with context and domain. But can we say more than that? It seems clear, for example, that he wants the use of contraceptives and intimate consensual sexual relationships to be protected. But what else? I may feel that my choice of profession is part of my definition of myself, part of my self-identity, and a way in which I express myself and my individuality, for example. But is that choice, and the relationships associated with it, the sort of thing that should be protected as private? For those who think not, Schoeman's notion of individual self-expression needs to be narrowed or clarified.

Another question arises when we reconsider Schoeman's thesis that privacy shields people from *inappropriate* manifestations of social pressure. He urges that what counts as *overreaching* interference will vary, but are there no clearer guidelines? Probably most of us share similar intuitions on a wide range of cases as to what sort of pressure or interference we would view as inappropriate. But inevitably controversial cases arise. How much social pressure or interference can one legitimately bring to bear on a woman's decision whether or not to have an abortion? Is this not just another way of asking the question of whether privacy protects that woman's decision? Does discussing legitimate and illegitimate interference and social pressure help us answer the privacy question in that case, or does it merely move it to a different level? Appropriate and inappropriate social pressure or interference within different contexts need to be distinguished. Otherwise, the characterization is too broad.

Consider also a different type of case. Recalling informational concerns usually categorized as core privacy issues, we might wonder how they are to be understood on Schoeman's analysis. Academic and medical information, for example, is protected by the Privacy Act of 1974, and most of us believe that such information, as well as information about our financial and credit status, is information we would like protected as private because we feel vulnerable to its potential appropriation and misuse. But despite that vulnerability, is it information that helps enhance our self-expression and thus deserving of privacy protection? Or is this information to be understood as private because it is protected by social norms and taboos already rigidly defined by our culture? Neither explanation seems entirely satisfactory to me, and so while I feel confident that Schoeman would include this information in the realm of the private, I am unsure how he would account for that inclusion. It would be helpful to know how expressive-role privacy relates to more traditional privacy interests. Schoeman's approach makes progress in answering controversial questions about the scope and value of privacy. Nevertheless, it is still incomplete.

Three Aspects of Privacy

My account of privacy attempts to answer these questions raised by Schoeman's discussion (and the theories of others). I argue that privacy is best understood as a cluster concept covering multiple privacy interests, including those enhancing control over information and our need for independence as well as those enhancing our ability to be self-expressive and to form social relationships. The cluster comprises three aspects of privacy, developed from standard explanations of core privacy concerns and supplemented with Schoeman's themes; they are related based on the historical links, linguistic usage, and similarity of justification that I have articulated. When this description is combined with a practical strategy for evaluating when a privacy intrusion is inappropriate and when an infringement of privacy can be justified, we can address the problem of accounting for justifiable invasions of privacy. I adopt the view that there is a presumption in favor of the need to protect privacy in the types of cases or contexts identified as those where privacy is at stake: that is, where it is reasonable to believe interference by others is illegitimate because of the ways it makes us vulnerable. That presumption can be rebutted, but arguments must be given to justify the public safety values or other claims that override the presumption. Note that Schoeman's defense of privacy emphasizes a theme brought out in the first chapter, namely that conceptions of privacy are likely to be extremely varied cross-culturally. My own characterization may ultimately be applicable in a wide range of cultures, but my discussion develops in a way that is self-consciously limited to contemporary American society.

It is clear from the discussion thus far that privacy acts as a shield to protect us in various ways, and its value lies in the freedom and independence it provides for us. Privacy shields us not only from interference and pressures that preclude self-expression and the development of relationships, as Schoeman emphasizes, but also from intrusions and pressures arising from others' access to our persons and details about us. Threats of information leaks as well as threats of control over our bodies, our activities, and our power to make our own choices give rise to fears that we are being scrutinized, judged, ridiculed, pressured, coerced, or otherwise taken advantage of by others. Protection of privacy enhances and ensures the freedom from such scrutiny, pressure to conform, and exploitation that we require so that as self-conscious beings we can maintain our self-respect, develop our self-esteem, and increase our ability to form a coherent identity and set of values, as well as our ability to form varied and complex relationships with others.[10] The realm of the private thus encompasses the types of information and activity that a reasonable person, in normal circumstances and under relevant social conventions, would view as illegitimate concerns of others owing to the threat of such constraining scrutiny, prejudice, judgment, and coercion.

One way of identifying the types of information and activity in which individuals might reasonably expect others not to interfere is to characterize aspects of privacy. Following Schoeman's suggestion that we can best understand privacy by examining the contexts where privacy arises or is a concern, I focus on three aspects of privacy. Each identifies overlapping clusters of privacy claims, types of information or activity for which a presumption in favor of privacy protection is reasonable, and contexts where privacy can provide a critical shield for us.

Informational privacy. Plainly there is nearly universal agreement that tort and Fourth Amendment privacy concerns characterized as control over information about oneself do constitute a basic core of privacy issues.[11] It is reasonable for people to have an expectation that under normal circumstances (barring, for example, cases where an individual is running for public political office) much information about themselves, personal or mundane, need not be available for public perusal. Thus information about one's daily activities, personal lifestyle, finances, medical history, and academic achievement, whether written or not, part of a public record or not, may be viewed by an individual as information he or she need not divulge and can expect others to guard as well. As we saw in chapter 2, individual privacy may be invaded by publication or even broader republication of such information; by intrusive snooping, observation, or wiretapping; by testing to gain or attempt to gain the information; or by surveillance. Such behavior can violate privacy whether or not information is actually recovered. The expectation of privacy is grounded in the fear concerning how the information might be used or appropriated to pressure or embarrass one, to damage one's credibility or economic status, and so on. Informational privacy protection thus shields individuals from intrusions as the well as fear of threats of intrusions, and it also affords individuals control in deciding who has access to the information and for what purposes.

Informational privacy addresses tort privacy concerns as described by Warren and Brandeis, articulated by William Prosser, and developed through later cases as described in chapter 1, as well as Fourth Amendment privacy protection of one's papers, letters, and effects. It is compatible with Alan Westin's definition of privacy as a "claim of individuals, groups, or institutions to determine for themselves when, how, and to what extent information about them is communicated to others."[12] Yet it is presented here as just one part of privacy, not a comprehensive definition.

Accessibility privacy. This aspect of privacy overlaps with informational privacy in cases where acquisition or attempted acquisition of information involves gaining access to an individual. But accessibility privacy also extends to cases where gaining information is not relevant but physical access is nevertheless at stake. The type of privacy concerns relevant here are those emphasized by Ruth Gavison and captured by her extended definition: "Privacy is a limitation of others' access to an individual. . . . [An] individual enjoys *perfect* privacy when he is completely inaccessible to others. . . . [I]n perfect privacy no one has any information about X, no one pays attention to X, and no one has physical access to X."[13] On my account, however, accessibility privacy focuses not merely on information or knowledge but more centrally on observations and physical proximity.

Protection of accessibility privacy allows one seclusion for behavior that social norms already prescribe as private, such as sexual and bathroom activities. But such privacy can also be undermined by physical closeness or surveillance in public and private spaces, or by access to individuals through the other senses, causing fear of overbearing scrutiny. Even surveillance of normal, everyday activities can lead one to be distracted and to feel inhibited. Such behavior can intrude on one's solitude or seclusion even if it is not yet noticed or discovered, because of the fear its potential recognition can generate. The damage that can be caused by the fear of being under surveillance cannot be underestimated: hence the stringent justifications and requirements that have historically been necessary for governmental surveillance to be allowed. Protection of accessibility privacy allows individuals to control decisions about who has physical access to their persons through sense perception, observation, or bodily contact and to limit access that would be unwelcome to reasonable individuals in the circumstances due to the distraction, inhibition, fear, and vulnerability it can cause.

Expressive privacy. Here privacy protects a realm for expressing one's self-identity or personhood through speech or activity. It protects the ability to decide to continue or to modify one's behavior when the activity in question helps define oneself as a person, shielded from interference, pressure, and coercion from government or from other individuals. Self-expression is critical for self-regarding acts of the type Mill described, as well as for intimate relationships, reproductive and family issues, and lifestyle choices that help define oneself and one's values—what Tribe calls the outward-looking dimension of privacy.[14] The extant constitutional cases give a beginning for identifying contexts where information and behavior may be presumed to be private in this sense, but only a beginning. For the Court has said that constitutional privacy protects "fundamental" decisions, and we have seen that this is inadequate in its vagueness.

While one's political or religious commitments or career concerns may not be intimate, they may well be relevant to one's development of self-identity in a way that makes it reasonable to expect that choices and activities related to those commitments be viewed as presumptively private. I am inclined toward the inclusive view that allows recognition of such concerns as private, though these may be more likely than others to be overridden by considerations of public safety or harm to other persons. I would thus interpret the notion of self-expression broadly at this initial stage of identifying privacy concerns. Privacy will actually be protected when it survives the second-stage evaluation determining that an invasion is not justifiable.

Expressive privacy, as Schoeman argues persuasively, limits external social control over choices about lifestyle and enhances internal control over self-expression and the ability to build interpersonal relationships. Gavison explains, "Privacy . . . prevents interference, pressures to conform, ridicule, punishment, unfavorable decisions, and other forms of hostile reaction. To the extent privacy does this, it functions to promote liberty of action, removing the unpleasant consequences of certain actions and thus increasing the liberty to perform them."[15] But on my view this describes just one of three types of privacy claims. This aspect of privacy reflects Stevens's language in *Whalen* that privacy encompasses protection of an "interest in independence in making certain kinds of important decisions" and covers Tom Gerety's definition of privacy as "control over the intimacies of personal identity."[16] It is also in accordance with the Court's wording elsewhere embracing self-definition: it is the type of privacy at stake in the constitutional cases where the Court has protected decisions by families in the areas of reproductive control (*Griswold, Eisenstadt, Roe*), schooling (*Pierce*), and lifestyle (*Loving, Stanley*).[17] In such cases privacy protects one from the fears of pressure to conform, from being coerced to hold homogenized viewpoints, and from being harassed or damaged by the stigmatization of one's choices. For these reasons expressive privacy is conceptually linked with the other two aspects of privacy.

The account I have given treats privacy not merely as a two-pronged type of protection covering tort and constitutional cases, but as a complex of three related clusters of claims concerning information about oneself, physical access to oneself, and decision making and activity that provide one with the independence needed to carve out one's self-identity through self-expression and interpersonal relationships. Each can be viewed as reflecting Warren and Brandeis's concern to protect individual personhood and "inviolate personality," Westin's insistence on protection of "individuality" and the "core self," and the protection identified in *Pavesich* and in *Botsford* as the inviolability of the person. This characterization also reflects the Supreme Court's recognition, emphasized by Ronald Dworkin in his book *Life's Dominion*, of the various ways that bodily integrity has been held to form an important component of privacy.[18]

I cannot claim that this set of clusters is fully exhaustive of privacy claims, although I believe it must be close. I realize as well that this complex description may not satisfy those desiring a unified and simple account of privacy. However, such desires are misplaced: as we have seen, narrow and unitary definitions in law and philosophy are inadequate. Note, in addition, that my tripartite account of privacy allows for further explication in law such as other concepts have undergone as they have developed. One commentator has pointed out, for example, that even a positivist like H. L. A. Hart, in discussing when sanctions should apply to people who fail to exercise reasonable care to avoid injury to others, realized in his later work that "there are clear cases where this standard applies and clear cases where it does not, but in large measure precisely which cases are covered by the standards cannot be known prior to determination by the court. Courts are left to determine whether the burden of proper precaution does or does not involve too great a sacrifice of others' interests in order to avoid substantial harm."[19] In such cases the law can be consistent and rational while evolving to adapt to social and technological change.

My characterization of these three aspects of privacy gives a comprehensive overview of privacy as an important value that provides a shield for us in a variety of contexts. But it is only useful when augmented with a strategy for practical moral and legal assessment. The strategy I endorse is to begin with a *presumption* of a reasonable expectation of privacy in the contexts and types of cases I have described, while acknowledging that social, legal, and moral considerations may require that the presumption be overridden. The task, then, for legislators, judges, and moral and political theorists is to work out ways to maintain and enhance privacy, or provide the rationale for when and why a privacy presumption can be overridden, determining when a privacy invasion is justifiable, even if the context is normally viewed as a private one. Some cases will be clear. Child abuse and wife battering cannot be condoned even if they occur in the privacy of one's home. On other cases certainly many will disagree, as will become clear in subsequent chapters. What I am defending, however, is the importance of the view that the disagreement focus on the *stringency* of the privacy claim as it is weighed and balanced against other individual and social concerns, not on the question about whether or not there *is* a privacy interest at stake at all.

In chapter 5 I address and respond to the feminist critique of privacy. I then demonstrate the implications of defending privacy as a concept with broad scope in reproductive and sexual contexts in chapters 6 and 7, highlighting ways that my account helps explain and refocus current debates on privacy and morality. Chapters 8 and 9 illustrate the importance and benefits of adopting my presumptive strategy, especially for applications where technological advance raises new issues about how extensively to protect privacy. While I cannot evaluate the justifiable balance in every case, and cannot generalize a rule describing when intrusion by others is overbearing or inappropriate, I provide models for finding an acceptable balance. Placing presumptive weight on privacy is a strategy that can provide standards for maintaining privacy protection in the face of developing technologies.

I have not provided a constitutional defense for citing privacy as one right at stake in the *Griswold* line of cases.[20] Nor have I attempted to enter the debate about how strictly to interpret the Constitution. Yet I have demonstrated that there are strong reasons to agree that there is an interest in privacy at issue in these constitutional cases. The implications of defending a broad conception of privacy are significant. Current constitutional standards, controversial though they may be, require "strict scrutiny" by the Court for cases concerning "fundamental values," and privacy has been judged one such value. Thus these privacy claims have a *greater* chance of being protected when they conflict with other rights or general interests than they would have if only liberty, or freedom from governmental interference, were involved.

The Feminist Critique
of Privacy

As we have seen, there has been extensive debate among philosophers and legal theorists about what privacy means, whether and how it can be defined, and the scope of protection it can and should afford. Reactions to recent Supreme Court confirmation hearings have made it clear that many in the public and in Congress are unwilling to give up the privacy protection they currently enjoy. They view privacy, as I do, as a valuable shield for protecting a sphere within which we can act free of scrutiny and intrusion by others.

In contrast, many feminists have called attention to the "darker side of privacy," citing its potential to shield domination, repression, degradation, and physical harm to women and others without power. It might be thought that this feminist critique of privacy is powerful enough to defeat my thesis that we can and must view privacy as a meaningful concept with significant value for a wide range of claims associated with tort, Fourth Amendment, and other constitutional law. I argue in this chapter, to the contrary, that we may support many concerns raised by the feminist critique of privacy without abandoning the concept of privacy and the significant benefits a strong right of privacy affords.

Perhaps the most prominent version of this critique of privacy is articulated by Catharine MacKinnon. She begins by observing that

the idea of privacy embodies a tension between precluding public exposure or governmental intrusion on the one hand, and autonomy in the sense of protecting personal self-action on the other. This is a tension, not just two facets of one right. The liberal state resolves this tension by identifying the threshold of the state at its permissible extent of penetration into a domain that is considered free by definition: the private sphere. By this move the state secures "an inviolable personality" by ensuring "autonomy of control over the intimacies of personal identity."[1] The state does this by centering its self-restraint on body and home, especially bedroom. By staying out of marriage and the family—essentially meaning sexuality, that is, heterosexuality—from contraception through pornography to the abortion decision, the law of privacy proposes to guarantee individual bodily integrity, personal exercise of moral intelligence, and freedom of intimacy. But have women's rights to access to those values been guaranteed? The law of privacy instead translates traditional liberal values into the rhetoric of individual rights as a means of subordinating those rights to specific social imperatives.[2]

MacKinnon is of course correct that privacy has developed in law to protect both (i) an "individual interest in avoiding disclosure of personal matters," as well as limiting governmental intrusion on and regulation of these matters, and (ii) an "interest in independence in making certain kinds of important decisions" regarding body, home, and lifestyle.[3] Many legal theorists have taken these to be clearly separable interests, whereas I have argued in earlier chapters that there are deeper similarities and connections between the two than is usually acknowledged.[4] Following most legal theorists, MacKinnon treats protection from public exposure and governmental intrusion as separate from and in tension with protection of autonomous decision making. Perhaps her reason is that she finds these goals incompatible: safeguarding (i) precludes guaranteeing (ii).

A serious difficulty, MacKinnon believes, is that the state merges these two interests by drawing the line where state intrusion is no longer justified at those matters concerning body, home, and the heterosexual family, asserting that in this way it is protecting personal autonomy. But, MacKinnon continues, the move to ensure autonomy in intimate relations with respect to the body, home, and family relations does nothing to help women, since the values of individual bodily integrity, exercise of moral intelligence, and freedom of intimacy are not guaranteed to women. The fundamental flaw, according to MacKinnon, is that underlying privacy protection in the law is a liberal ideal of the private: as long as the public does not interfere, autonomous individuals interact freely and equally. But this presumes that women are, like men, free and equal, an assumption MacKinnon finds patently false. When the private is defined as personal, intimate, autonomous, and individual, it is on her view defined by reference to characteristics most feminists believe women do not possess. The law of privacy thus presumes a liberal conception of rights with false assumptions about women. Moreover, privacy is just one instance where our legal system fails to recognize and take into account the preexisting oppression and inequality of women. For MacKinnon, privacy represents yet another domain where women are deprived of power and are deprived of recourse under the law, all on the suspect theory that "the government best promotes freedom when it stays out of existing social relationships."[5]

MacKinnon continues her argument in even stronger language:

For women the measure of the intimacy has been the measure of the oppression. This is why feminism has had to explode the private. This is why feminism has seen the personal as the political. The private is public for those for whom the personal is political. In this sense, for women there is no private, either normatively or empirically. Feminism confronts the fact that women have no privacy to lose or to guarantee. Women are not inviolable. Women's sexuality is not only violable, it is—hence, women are—seen in and as their violation. To confront the fact that women have no privacy is to confront the intimate degradation of women as the public order. The doctrinal choice of privacy in the abortion context thus reaffirms and reinforces what the feminist critique of sexuality criticizes: the public/private split.[6]

MacKinnon appears to be making two distinct but related claims here. The first is that women have no privacy, and hence protecting privacy provides no benefit at all for women. Privacy protection may even be a positive detriment to women, giving men the legal right to treat their wives and partners (and children) unequally or even brutally.[7] The second claim is that feminism has demonstrated the importance of criticizing the split between public and private domains, and thus "has had to explode the private." Let us consider each in turn.

Why is it that women have no privacy to lose or guarantee? MacKinnon's answer appears to be that because women are violable and violated, they have no zone of autonomy within which to control their destinies. In particular, in the realm of sexuality, often viewed as a paradigmatic example of the private, women do not have control. Men can and often do maintain their power over women in such intimate circumstances. Although sexual intimacy, and activities within the home and family, may be private in the sense of being withheld from public view and shielded from governmental intrusion, they are not private in the sense of being areas where women have control over their decision making.

This argument is easily refuted. Note first that I have already shown, contrary to MacKinnon, that although privacy law does in part protect one's ability to make intimate and personal choices, it does not follow that privacy is merely equivalent to autonomy or control over decision making. Privacy and autonomy are distinct concepts and can and should be differentiated.[8] Second, even if women do in fact often lose control in the domain of intimate sexual relations, it does not follow that they have no interest in the value of protecting a zone for autonomous decision making. MacKinnon often repeats her claim that women have no privacy that can be taken away. That women are in fact violated in private contexts, however, implies nothing about the worth of protecting a zone within which they can have the power to limit intrusions and violations. In short, descriptive facts about actual limitations on privacy fail to imply anything about the normative value of seeking privacy protection for women.

MacKinnon's second point in this passage underscores the importance of rejecting the public/private split. The public/private distinction has captured the imagination of many feminist scholars. In fact a substantial portion of feminist theory and political struggle over the past two hundred years has been concerned with deconstructing the traditional notion, going back as far as Aristotle, of a public (male) political realm and a private (female) domestic realm.[9] Some of the most influential work in feminist political theory, philosophy, and legal theory takes this paradigm as its starting point in analyzing women's oppression. Carole Pateman goes so far as to claim that the public/private dichotomy "is, ultimately, what the feminist movement is about."[10] Yet despite this emphasis on the public/private distinction, it is difficult to clarify what the feminist critique of it entails. Feminist scholars such as Ruth Gavison and Pateman have made clear that there is no single or privileged version.[11] There are, to the contrary, a multiplicity of interwoven ways of understanding attacks on the public/private dichotomy. As regards MacKinnon in particular, it is not clear what she means by the need to "explode" the private. She appears to believe there is no distinction between public and private because there is no private realm for women at all. Does she also mean to say that there *should* be no public/private distinction?

In part MacKinnon is, like other prominent feminists, drawing attention to the degree to which sexual and physical violence in the family has been a degrading and life-altering experience for so many women. She is surely correct that abusive relationships in those traditionally private contexts are pervasive. To the extent that the private or domestic sphere is held unavailable for public scrutiny, abuse and degradation can continue unchecked. When there are legal avenues for women to combat abuse, the system often does not or cannot enforce them effectively.[12] Moreover, on MacKinnon's view, both the public and private spheres exhibit the social power of sexism. The subordination of women to men is evident in public, and in private it is mirrored and allowed to run its course, "inaccessible to, unaccountable to . . . anything beyond itself."[13] Thus privacy as currently defended keeps women isolated and politically powerless. Characterizing a realm of domestic, personal, intimate, and familial relations as private sustains and increases existing unfair power relationships and opportunities for abuse. Hence the separation of "public" and "private" obscures the damaging effects of perpetuating oppression of women and is intensely detrimental to women.

I believe we can agree with MacKinnon that whenever distinguishing public and private realms renders the domestic arena unsuitable for scrutiny, then the distinction works to the detriment of women. But what is the alternative? If the line between public and private is sometimes indeterminate, does it follow that nothing is or should be private? If there is no distinction between public and private, is everything public? Should every part of our lives be open to public appraisal? Indeed, on one interpretation of MacKinnon's view that we must "explode" the public/private distinction and that "the private is public," we must totally reject any realm of the private and apparently must conclude that everything is public. Thus rejection of the dichotomy is accomplished by collapsing the private into the public. Others have viewed this as a plausible reading of the feminist critique of privacy. For example, in a recent discussion of the public and private, Jean Bethke Elshtain describes one form of the feminist critique:

In its give-no-quarter form in radical feminist argument, any distinction between the personal and the political was disdained. Note that the claim was not that the personal and political are interrelated in ways previously hidden by male-dominated political ideology and practice, or that the personal and political might be analogous to each other along certain axes of power and privilege. Rather, there was a collapse of one into the other: The personal *is* political. Nothing personal was exempt from political definition, direction, and manipulation—not sexual intimacy, not love, not parenting. The total collapse of public and private as central distinctions in an enduring democratic drama followed, at least in theory.

The private sphere fell under a thoroughgoing politicized definition. Everything was grist for a voracious publicity mill; nothing was exempt, there was nowhere to hide.[14]

A similar understanding of the feminist critique of privacy is echoed by Ruth Gavison, who observes, "Usually, when the dichotomy between public and private is challenged, the argument is that all is (or should be) public." Yet Gavison quickly notes that feminists often equivocate when confronted with the implications of this rejection of the public/private split:

> But once we look at particular questions, it is rare to find feminists who argue consistently either that everything should be regulated by the state, or that the family and all other forms of intimate relationships should disappear in favor of public communities that . . . police the different ways in which members interact. When pushed, feminists explicitly deny this is their ideal. . . . [I]t is hard to specify even one context or dimension of the distinction in which the claim is that the whole category of the private is useless.[15]

Thus, even if women are often vulnerable and exploited in the private, domestic sphere, we may ask whether it follows that women have *no* interest in values of accessibility privacy as freedom from intrusion and expressive privacy as control over certain intimate and personal decisions and relationships. Are there *no* contexts in which women wish to keep the state out of their lives? MacKinnon often writes as if she would respond affirmatively, especially in her argument against privacy protection and in favor of equality analysis in feminist jurisprudence.[16] Nevertheless, I suspect the answer must be no, even for MacKinnon. Anita Allen has suggested that an analogy between privacy and liberty is helpful here. Just as the harm that results from the exercise of individual liberty does not lead to the rejection of liberty, similarly there is inadequate reason to reject privacy completely based on harm done in private.[17]

MacKinnon believes that the public/private distinction perpetuates the subjection of women in the domestic sphere, encouraging a policy of nonintervention by the state. She seems then to be making a further point as well: that male power over women is affirmatively embodied in privacy law. In the words of Susan Moller Okin, "The protection of the privacy of a domestic sphere in which inequality exists is the protection of the right of the strong to exploit and abuse the weak."[18] Batterers and child molesters rely on the shroud of secrecy that surrounds abuse to maintain their power. Thus many have worked to make the state more responsive to the abuse of women by rejecting legal privacy protection for the family. MacKinnon concludes,

> The right of privacy is a right of men "to be let alone" to oppress women one at a time. It embodies and reflects the private sphere's existing definition of womanhood. This instance of liberalism—applied to women as if they were persons, gender neutral—reinforces the division between public and private which is not gender neutral. It is an ideological division that lies about women's shared experience. . . . It polices the division between public and private, a very material division that keeps the private beyond public redress and depoliticizes women's subjection within it.[19]

The insights of this critique of privacy underscore how important it is to take care when viewing public and private categories differently. Feminists have correctly identified the ways in which the distinction can be dangerous if it is used to devalue the work of women in domestic roles, to silence them politically by categorizing them as having no public voice or value, and to allow the continuation of abuse and degradation under the cover of a private sphere unavailable for public censure. Thus MacKinnon and other feminists are right to urge that the distinction not be used to justify differential social and legal treatment of women. The "privacy" of the family, for example, should not be invoked to mask exploitation and battering of family members.

On one hand, it seems clear that defenders of privacy have too often ignored the role of *individual* male power, and sexual and physical abuse, in domestic contexts. On the other hand, focus on domestic violence ignores *state-sponsored* expressions of control over women. Consider, for example, intrusions such as government sterilization programs and the interventions involved in state control over welfare programs, including the withdrawal of benefits from women upon the birth of additional children.[20]

Consequently, this first interpretation of MacKinnon's sweeping critique may ultimately lead to a view stronger than she means to endorse. Rejecting the public/private distinction in this way obscures the difference between individual and institutional expressions of (male) power. On this reading, MacKinnon highlights the very real existence of domination by individual men over women, then argues for the rejection of privacy, and thereby implies everything should remain public. In doing so, she fails to address the need to differentiate between justified and unjustified uses of state power over individuals.[21] Governmental regulation might refer to reasonable laws regarding family matters, such as giving women the right to charge husbands with rape. Or it might mean that the state will reveal and regulate all the embarrassing details. There is, moreover, an important difference between a government that protects a woman's decision to charge her husband with rape and one that forces her to do so. Evaluating the justifiability of state intervention requires specifying what kind of regulation is at issue.[22] We may decry violations of women by individual men, and may well defend the role of the state to intervene—reasonably, firmly, and effectively—given evidence of domestic violence. Exploitation and abuse *should* be matters of public concern. But that need not imply that there is never value in making a distinction between public and private. We need not be committed to the view that there should be *no* limitations on state interference in individual, personal, and intimate affairs. We need not be pushed to agree that there should be *no* private realm within which women can live their lives free from state policing and intrusion.

In short, on this first interpretation of her critique of privacy, MacKinnon correctly emphasizes the need to limit individual violations and intrusions on women by men, but at the same time she underemphasizes the need to limit intrusions by the state. We can agree with her about the oppression and inequality of women, the reality and pervasiveness of abuse, and the dangers of distinguishing a private domestic realm immune from public scrutiny that preserves the status quo. Yet we can disagree with the view that there is never value in differentiating public and private spheres, and we can appreciate the importance of restricting governmental power over individual men and women. Women have a stake in the preservation of privacy despite the fact that it can be a source of danger to them. The difficult political, legal, and philosophical issues include the practical problems of gathering evidence of abuse and differentiating when state intervention is appropriate and when it is not. To the extent that we can address them, we can confront the "darker side of privacy" without leaving our personal lives entirely vulnerable to intrusion by others.

Some may believe, however, that this first interpretation of MacKinnon's argument is unsympathetic and actually misses a central point of the feminist critique of privacy. Other readers of MacKinnon's critique dispute the view that rejecting the public/private split merely collapses one side of the dichotomy onto the other.[23] On this alternative interpretation, that is neither the feminist point nor an implication of the feminist position. To the contrary, feminists want to do away with the whole public/private dichotomy *as it has been understood in the past.* Thus feminists stress that they do not intend to have the state insinuating itself into the most intimate parts of people's lives. They are instead emphasizing that the state must stop ignoring the unbelievable abuses that have been protected in the name of privacy; this is, they believe, a position that is not captured by the public/private distinction as it has been known and used. According to this account, whether or not it is successfully captured by MacKinnon, feminists are talking about a position that bypasses the public/private distinction in a different way.

For example, Frances Olsen discusses the radical separation of two spheres of activity: the (public) market and (private) family, and their relationship to two other dichotomies, between state and civil society and between male and female. Olsen describes strategies for improving the status of women, including legal reforms addressing both the family and the market. She argues, however, that such strategies, intended to promote equal treatment and antidiscrimination, have ultimately had destructive effects. These include perpetuating the continuous and systematic economic and social subordination of women, in part because of the unequal bargaining power of women compared to men. She insists,

as long as we view market and family as a dichotomy, our ideal images of market and family will remain incomplete and unsatisfactory. . . . The reforms that make the family more like the market and the market more like the family likewise do not overcome the dichotomy between market and family but presuppose it. Although these reforms might appear to be a step toward transcending the market/family dichotomy, experience with such reforms suggests a persistent tendency simply to reproduce in each sphere the failures as well as the successes of the other.[24]

Olsen urges that the public/private and market/family dichotomies are a way of thinking, a human creation; they are a prism through which we have come to experience our lives. It is not enough to recognize the crippling effects of such dichotomies. "Dividing life between market and family compartmentalizes human experience in a way that prevents us from realizing the range of choices actually available to us" (81).

Clearly Olsen is not endorsing the first interpretation of MacKinnon's rejection of the public/private split. She points out that many believe criticism of the separation of market and family will lead to an alternative system in which "the state controls every aspect of human life; nothing is personal and private" (83)—and she emphatically rejects this implication, saying she does not advocate replacing the present dichotomies with an all-powerful state. Instead, Olsen urges that we neither reject the humanization and connectedness of the family nor the efficient production of goods and services in the market. It is their separation and polarization that reinforces the status quo and limits possibilities of human association. On her view, "We cannot choose between the two sides of the dualism because we need both" (88). The preferable alternative is to transcend the dichotomies in some yet-to-be-articulated way, preserving a meaningful role for an important concept of privacy.

Carole Pateman reiterates the feminist challenge to the separation and opposition between public and private spheres as central categories of political liberalism, where domestic family life is paradigmatically private. Pateman believes that "the dichotomy between the private and the public obscures the subjection of women to men within an apparently universal, egalitarian and individualist order. . . . The essential feminist argument is that the doctrine of 'separate but equal,' and the ostensible individualism and egalitarianism of liberal theory, obscure the patriarchal reality of a social structure of inequality and the domination of women by men."[25] But she emphasizes that feminists reject the claim that a public/private dichotomy is inevitable:

They [feminists] argue that a proper understanding of liberal social life is possible only when it is accepted that the two spheres, the domestic (private) and civil society (public) held to be separate and opposed, are inextricably interrelated; they are the two sides of the single coin of liberal-patriarchialism. . . . [Furthermore,] feminist critiques insist that an alternative to the liberal conception must also encompass the relationship between public and domestic life.[26]

What is needed, on Pateman's view, is a feminist theoretical perspective that takes account of social relationships between men and women within the context of interpretations of both the public and the private. Work by political theorists such as John Stuart Mill,[27] as well as practical experience from the feminist movement, has shown that women's place in the private sphere cannot simply be augmented by extending to women a role in the public sphere. The spheres are not additive but integrally related. As Pateman notes, "These feminist critiques of the dichotomy between private and public stress that the categories refer to two *interrelated* dimensions of the structure of liberal-patriarchalism; they do not necessarily suggest that no distinction can or should be drawn between the personal and political aspects of social life" (emphasis mine).[28] In sum, Pateman views the feminist critique of privacy as stressing rejection of the dichotomy *as it has been understood*, but she concludes that the "separate" worlds of private and public life are closely interrelated and that both are necessary dimensions of a future, democratic feminist social order. An adequate account, after acknowledging that public and private are not necessarily in harmony, will develop a social theory in which these categories are distinct but interrelated, rather than totally separate or opposed.

Pateman's approach also highlights another dimension of feminist perspectives on the public/private split. The well-known slogan "the personal is political" is often taken to be one of feminism's most significant lessons. Whom one sleeps with, whether one has an abortion, whether one seeks reproduction-assisting technologies, whether one is a religious fundamentalist, and so on—all these choices have political implications. Moreover, personal circumstances and family life are regulated and structured by public factors, including legislation concerning rape and sexuality, marriage and divorce, and policies on child care and welfare. What feminists are trying to articulate in this strand of argument is that the public/private dichotomy is misleading in critical ways because it fails to reflect the interconnections between public and private.

In a similar recognition of interconnections, a further dimension of the feminist critique of privacy to which MacKinnon alludes focuses on the communal aspects of individual actions. This account stresses that it is not merely *individual* men's abuse of women but the *social and cultural* aspects of male violence that must be recognized and addressed. Its proponents point to a growing body of empirical literature on male bonding that indicates ever more clearly that we live to a certain extent in a "rape culture," which continues to encourage male bonding around the abuse of women. Hence, what must be emphasized is not private male violence against women as a problem of individual men, but the importance of accounting for male violence against women as a far more encompassing public social problem.

Clearly the feminist critique of privacy is multifaceted, and there is no question that Olsen and Pateman acknowledge the difficulties of the public/private dichotomy and the damaging effects of accepting it as it has been defended in the past. Both, however, appear to agree that absent domination and abuse, there may be great value for women as well as men in preserving a sanctuary where we can live free from scrutiny and the pressure to conform, free to express our identities through relationships and choices about our bodies and lifestyles, without government intrusion. Nevertheless, this clearly leads to a challenge for Olsen and Pateman, as well as other feminists like Gavison, Allen, Elshtain, and myself, who are unwilling to jettison privacy completely. Given the lingering influence, in our culture and law, of the separate spheres analysis—that women belong in the home and men in public positions—it may take much time and effort to address the difficulties of preserving the two spheres in some form while extricating them from their gendered past and gendered connotations.[29] Perhaps MacKinnon believes that these difficulties are insurmountable.

It is now clear, however, that the feminist critique of privacy, on either of the interpretations I have examined, does not undermine my defense of a broad conception of privacy. Exploding the public/private distinction by collapsing it to leave all public is an unacceptable and even dangerous alternative, granting excessive power to the state. While we may often find it difficult to determine when official intervention is warranted, defending privacy as a shield to ward off unjustified individual and institutional intrusions in our personal lives remains an essential component of both our moral and legal systems if we are to preserve both peace of mind and bodily integrity. Alternatively, recognizing the insidious effects of the dichotomy, including the continued subordination of women, and rejecting the distinction as it has been understood in the past are compatible with retaining a meaningful concept of privacy in a theory of a new social order as envisioned by such feminists as Olsen and Pateman.

Judicial Interpretation and John Hart Ely's Critique of *Roe v. Wade*

In this chapter I address an implication of construing privacy broadly: defending its importance and relevance in the constitutional privacy cases, especially the famous 1973 abortion decision, *Roe v. Wade*.[1] *Roe v. Wade* is certainly taken to be one of the most controversial of the constitutional privacy cases decided by the Supreme Court. In their efforts to attack *Roe*, many have aimed their criticism at privacy as a legal concept as well as the dominant role it plays in the Court's opinion. Such criticisms are sometimes open to a quick rebuttal. Some have claimed, for example, that privacy cannot be at stake in the case since abortions are usually performed in the presence of one or more individuals, including nurses and doctors. But that argument relies on interpreting privacy as secrecy or concealment, a definition I criticized and rejected in chapter 3.

A more serious concern, as noted in chapter 2, is the argument that because the term "privacy" appears nowhere in the Constitution, there can be no constitutional right to privacy. We shall see this rests on an untenable theory of judicial adjudication. In addition, over twenty years after *Roe*, John Hart Ely's famous *Yale*

Law Journal essay, "The Wages of Crying Wolf: A Comment on *Roe v. Wade*," is still widely viewed as its most penetrating and devastating critique.[2] Thus we might well wonder whether Ely's critique undermines my view that there is a meaningful and legitimate notion of privacy at stake in that case. In fact, it is possible to understand Ely's major critique in a way that is compatible with recognizing a woman's right to privacy in the abortion context. My interpretation of the focus of his argument illuminates the decision in this crucial privacy case, although it certainly does not resolve disputes between those defending different positions on the abortion question.

Constitutional Interpretation

There are a variety of views regarding the role of judges in constitutional decision making, and it will be helpful if we distinguish a few of these very roughly. A dominant theme in the American constitutional tradition is originalism, what Paul Brest calls "the familiar approach to constitutional adjudication that accords binding authority to the text of the Constitution or the intentions of its adopters."[3] One widely accepted justification for originalism is that the Constitution is the supreme law of the land and expresses the will of the citizens; hence the judge's task is to ascertain their collective will through a strict interpretation of the document. Originalism is often associated with legal positivism, and it underlies the view described by members of the Reagan administration, such as ex–Attorney General Edwin Meese, that judges must apply the law as it is stated to the facts presented to deduce the judgment.[4] The goal of originalism is to constrain judicial discretion and to avoid judicial activism so that unelected officials are not usurping the legislative function.

One version of originalism focuses on strict interpretation of the constitutional text, construing words and phrases narrowly and precisely. Defenders of this view might well be concerned to articulate the intentions of the framers of the Constitution, yet they believe the text is the surest guide for doing so. Unfortunately, most scholars agree that despite the appeal of the rhetoric in defense of such a view, a strict interpretation of the Constitution is problematic or impossible in many cases.[5] One major concern with strict textualism is that it is too dependent on history. It requires and relies on a difficult or perhaps impossible historical inquiry to understand how phrases such as "cruel and unusual punishment" were used at the time the Constitution was drafted and to determine the perspective of the adopters themselves.

More worrisome, there are many open-ended or vague phrases in the Constitution that cannot merely be applied straightforwardly. For example, what conduct counts as "free speech"? Does "equal protection of the law" grant Allan Bakke admission to medical school or exclude him in order to generate equal opportunity for minorities? And what is protected as "due process" under the Fourteenth Amendment? In none of these cases can the words merely be applied to facts to generate a decision. Even given historical information about eighteenth-century usage of the terms in the text, reading a provision without regard to its current social context may yield irresolvable indeterminacies, and the consistency hoped for may be elusive.

An alternative version of originalism, suggested by Robert Bork, Raoul Berger, and others, urges basing decisions in difficult cases on the intentions of the framers of the Constitution.[6] There are a number of serious difficulties with this view, similar to the problems with strict literalism. Again, it is a substantial historical project to ascertain the relevant intentions. The legal history of any legislation drafting often yields inconclusive or inconsistent testimony and evidence, making it difficult or sometimes impossible to discern the "true" intention of the framers. And new historical evidence can shed light on or actually alter an understanding of their "real" intent. Moreover, the task in this instance is a particularly complex one: the men who adopted the Constitution were a diverse group, including some delegates to the Philadelphia convention and the majorities in ratifying conventions. Perhaps some members had clear intentions about certain constitutional provisions, yet others may have held different views or may have had no clear intent. Hence it is not at all obvious how, or whether it is indeed possible, to determine their collective intent with any reliability.

In addition, this view of adjudication requires ascertaining the adopter's intentions not only about the meaning of various provisions but also about their scope, including what the adopters intended future interpreters to do. By this point, one may well be wondering why a historian's judgment about what was intended two hundred years ago should determine the legitimacy of a current interpretation. It is even more difficult to see how to project the adopters' concepts and attitudes onto a future radically different from their experience. When a case involves an issue that was not or could not have been anticipated by the framers, perhaps because of intervening technological or medical advances, there may be no way of determining their intentions: no information is available. Did the framers intend First Amendment protection for the mass media, for example? In such cases the theory either cannot be applied at all or must allow the kind of subjective judicial decision making it is constructed to avoid.

Most other legal theorists believe, therefore, that these narrow methods are unrealistic and often impossible to put into practice. In order to give content to the ambiguous and vague language of the Constitution and to allow the Constitution and governmental process to adapt to technological and social changes, some more active judicial interpretation of the law is necessary. Yet any such activisim feeds worries of a slippery slope. If judges have some discretion in interpreting the law, what constraints are they bound by? A genuine concern is that allowing some judicial discretion will lead to freewheeling judicial innovation, as described and defended by American legal realists in the early twentieth century. We might characterize their view as follows: all law is judge-made law, the judicial decision is the law, and legal rules are merely legal resources, not binding on judges. On this account judges not only do but should make law.[7] The most extreme version of this view, that judicial decisions are wholly subjective and personal and that written opinions are merely rationalizations, is intuitively jarring. Moreover, realism seems contrary to two democratic ideals: (i) that making subjective legislative policy is inappropriate for unelected officials on courts and (ii) that ex post facto law is illegitimate because citizens deserve fair warning when their behavior is beyond the bounds of law.

Clearly, a more acceptable view on the decision-making role of the judge will fall somewhere between originalism and extreme realism. There are a wide range of alternative views on the proper domain of judicial intervention. One requires judicial interpretation to be guided by some set of evolving principles, such as those suggested by Lon Fuller, principles that can be defended as embodied in the Constitution and its history because they focus on the goals and purposes of constitutional provisions.[8] Another example is Ronald Dworkin's rights-based constitutional theory, which incorporates into law moral principles that he argues are compatible with the institutional values of our government and its history.[9] Alexander Bickel appeals to broad "fundamental values," and Paul Brest defends a "nonoriginalism" view according to which "the text and original history of the Constitution get presumptive weight but are not treated as authoritative or binding; the presumption is defeasible over time in light of changing experience and perceptions."[10] John Hart Ely has taken a different route, advocating a process-oriented approach defending unrepresented minorities.[11]

These scholars may hold views more or less deferential to the legislature, more or less interventionist, but all expect judges to be constrained by rationality and consistency as far as possible and all place some weight on the Constitution as well as subsequent precedents. All endorse the view that, in Thomas Stoddard's words, "the principles of the Constitution should not be frozen in time, but should grow in meaning as the country evolves."[12] My arguments in preceding chapters lend themselves particularly well to the sort of background interpretation defended by Dworkin, perhaps supplemented by Dworkin's and Ely's accounts of courts functioning to protect unrepresented minorities. My purpose in this section is not to defend a particular mediating view on constitutional interpretation, however, but to stress the unacceptability of versions of originalism as theories of adjudication. It follows that it is implausible to reject the legitimacy of constitutional privacy on the grounds that it is not explicitly mentioned in the Constitution or was not intended by the framers.

Ely's Critique of *Roe v. Wade*

John Hart Ely begins "The Wages of Crying Wolf" by noting two criticisms of *Roe v. Wade* that he refers to as "standard." The first asserts that the Court could have used a narrower basis for the decision, such as the vagueness of the Texas abortion statute. On Ely's view the Court merely brushed that option aside. Second, Ely worries about the confusing signals emitted by the Court concerning doctors' responsibilities and the permissible scope of health regulations after the first trimester of pregnancy. But he finds neither of these issues serious enough to inspire a written commentary on the case.

Nor does Ely pursue some of the other criticism invited by Justice Harry Blackmun's wording in his majority opinion in *Roe v. Wade*. In particular, Blackmun may well have provided grounds (undoubtedly unintentionally) for responses such as the Human Life Amendments or Human Life Bills that have been submitted as attempts to overturn the *Roe* decision. Blackmun argued, "We need not resolve the difficult question of when life begins. When those trained in the respective disciplines of medicine, philosophy, and theology are unable to arrive at any consensus, the judiciary, at this point in the development of man's knowledge, is not in a position to speculate as to the answer."[13] Even if *at that point in the development of man's knowledge*, namely 1973, such a determination could not be expected, Blackmun's wording here invites critics to reply that *at some future time*, due to philosophical, medical, or other technological development or information, the judiciary *will* be in a position to try to make such a determination or to answer the difficult question about when life begins. Hence he encourages a dispute over the status of fetal life. Thus it was hardly surprising that during the Human Life Bill hearings nearly ten years later, testimony abounded from such experts about when life begins. Blackmun also wrote in *Roe v. Wade*, "in view of all this, we do not agree that, by adopting one theory of life, Texas may override the rights of the pregnant woman that are at stake."[14] Again the wording was less careful than it might have been. It leaves open the position that although the Court held that *Texas could not* adopt a certain theory of life in this way, it was at least not ruled out that *the federal government could do so* and could thereby override any rights of the mother. Yet although the sloppiness or lack of foresight in these unfortunate statements may explain some of the subsequent criticism of the case, such lapses are not sufficiently grievous to undermine the entire opinion.

Ely chooses instead to focus on a number of arguments far more serious than all of the concerns raised thus far, arguments that are intended to defend his claim that *Roe* is bad constitutional law. It is important to note that what makes his conclusion especially compelling is his insistence that he agrees politically with the outcome in the *Roe v. Wade* case. Early in his essay he asserts, "Let us not underestimate what is at stake: Having an unwanted child can go a long way toward ruining a woman's life. And at bottom *Roe* signals the Court's judgment that this result cannot be justified by any good that anti-abortion legislation accomplishes. This is surely an understandable conclusion—indeed it is one with which I agree."[15] A few pages later Ely restates the point somewhat differently: "Were I a legislator I would vote for a statute very much like the one the Court ends up drafting" (926). He hastens to point out that he is not *happy* with the resolution and that he believes the moral issue posed is one "as fiendish as any philosopher's hypothetical." Nevertheless, he makes clear his political sympathies with the result, despite his misgivings about its legal and constitutional justification.

Ely raises four somewhat interrelated criticisms of the *Roe* decision. All are important, yet I shall argue that the last is most central for Ely because of its link with his theory of adjudication. First, Ely begins with the claim that the Court should not be second-guessing the Texas legislature's balance of values as laid out in the anti-abortion statute in question. This argument in favor of deference to the legislature is a common one, though it has not always been determinative. Ely suggests that even if there are situations when it is reasonable for the Court to question the legislature's weighting of values, *Roe* is at the very least an odd case to choose. Such a move by the Court would be more compelling, according to Ely, in contexts concerning laws restricting drug use or consenting homosexuality, where there is no harm to any others beyond the participants. On Ely's view fetal life, whether the fetus is viewed as a person or not, makes the abortion decision distinctive from those other types of cases.

Second, Ely criticizes the Court's focus on viability as the point when protecting the fetus becomes a compelling state interest. It seems clear that Ely personally prefers quickening, the time at which the mother can first discern fetal movement, as a more reasonable cutoff. He suggests that quickening is historically more crucial than viability, yet he gives no defense for that claim. Ely worries in addition that viability is not a fixed target date, because technological advances can help sustain life at earlier and earlier points of development. But again he does not explain why that makes viability more objectionable than other cutoffs; some might even find it an appealing feature. Finally, Ely believes that the Court gives insufficient justification in the opinion for its choice of viability. All these criticisms are now well known, yet the Court majority has not rejected viability in its subsequent cases on abortion.

Ely stresses that for both of the foregoing arguments he believes it is irrelevant whether or not one views the fetus as a person, or even addresses or answers the question of personhood:

the argument that fetuses lack constitutional rights is simply irrelevant. For it has never been held or even asserted that the state interest needed to justify forcing a person to refrain from an activity, *whether or not that activity is constitutionally protected*, must implicate either the life or the constitutional rights of another person. Dogs are not "persons in the whole sense" nor have they constitutional rights, but that does not mean the state cannot prohibit killing them: It does not even mean the state cannot prohibit killing them in the exercise of the First Amendment right of political protest. Come to think of it, draft cards aren't persons either. (926)

Despite the perhaps inappropriate humor, Ely's serious point is clear: he will not enter into an argument over the status of fetal life, and he believes it is irrelevant whether or not one views the fetus as a person with constitutional rights. Ely insists repeatedly that the fetus may not be a person, but that it is not *nothing*, and thus there is in *Roe* an issue of harm.[16]

Third, Ely finds the *Roe v. Wade* decision worrisome because it relies neither on the intent of the framers of the Constitution nor on the governmental system contemplated by them. This critique does not invoke the criticism made by others that no right to privacy is written explicitly in the Constitution. Interestingly, Ely agrees that many constitutional amendments refer to privacy and he does not object to the earlier *Griswold v. Connecticut* case, which first announced and established a constitutional right to privacy. He goes so far as to say that it is entirely proper to infer a general right of privacy from the Constitution. Nevertheless, he does interpret the concept of privacy narrowly and believes that *Griswold* is justified on the grounds that enforcement of the statute against contraceptive information and use would have entailed outrageous governmental prying into the privacy of the home. Thus *Roe* is differentiable from *Griswold*, according to Ely, because it is not a case about governmental snooping.

Note that this argument merely assumes, but does not defend, a narrow view of privacy as concealment or protection from snooping. It is still possible to conceive of privacy broadly, as a meaningful concept for concerns over informational privacy, accessibility privacy, and expressive privacy linking personal issues of contraception use as well as reproductive control. A broad interpretation is compatible with Ely's argument, even if it was not developed and defended adequately by the Court. In addition, some have noted that it is difficult to discern a more principled basis for the view that privacy is relevant in *Griswold* but not *Roe*.[17] It is difficult to articulate compelling grounds for distinguishing control over sexual relations and control over changes within one's body. In fact, an important reason for viewing *Griswold* and *Roe* as conceptually intertwined is that the technologies of contraception and abortion overlap and over time will become more closely related.[18]

Fourth, Ely turns to what I take to be his central argument. Citing Justice Stone's famous footnote in the 1938 *United States v. Carolene Products* case,[19] Ely adopts Stone's suggestion about how extraordinary constitutional protection can be given for interests going beyond those expressed in the Constitution. Stone's idea was that the Court can specifically protect the interests of "discrete and insular minorities" unable to form political alliances. Ely believes that such a defense is consistent with the constitutional values envisioned by the framers and by the history of this country, even if it is nowhere expressed either in the Constitution itself or as an explicit reading of the framers' intentions. The brief explanation given by Ely in his essay is a summary of the theory of judicial decision making that he explains more fully and vigorously defends in his subsequent book, *Democracy and Distrust: A Theory of Judicial Review*. Ely not only endorses Stone's view but also argues that the theory it generates has had a strong effect on court decisions stressing equal treatment for women, who have inadequate political representation compared to men.

However, Ely continues, applying this theory to *Roe v. Wade* actually undermines the Court's decision. For Justice Stone's suggestion indicates that constitutional directive or not, the Court should throw its weight on the side of a minority demanding through legal action more than it has been able to achieve politically. That is, the Court can legitimately go beyond express protection written into the Constitution when it is protecting minorities unusually incapable of protecting themselves as compared to the interests of those to whom they have been subordinated. It is Ely's view that compared to men, women may well constitute such a political minority, even if there are numerically more women than men in the population. Compared to fetuses, however, women do not constitute such a minority. Ely asserts, "I'm not sure I'd know a discrete and insular minority if I saw one, but confronted with a multiple choice question requiring me to designate (a) women or (b) fetuses as one, I'd expect no credit for the former answer" (935).

Ely's concluding comments are more general. As a law professor and dean who once clerked for Supreme Court Chief Justice Earl Warren, Ely defends the controversial Warren Court decisions often labeled by critics as "activist" and as outrageous instances of subjective judicial decision making. He argues they are differentiable from *Roe* in part because they rely on protection of liberty as embodied in the Fourteenth Amendment, and because they can be defended using his theory of adjudication. Ely also compares *Roe* with the *Lochner* cases, a set of decisions from the early twentieth century in which the Court has been accused of baldly intruding into the arena of making legislative value judgments on a variety of issues such as work hours for women and children.[20] Like many other scholars, Ely views these cases as thoroughly disreputable. According to Ely, even though the *Lochner* cases concerned economic issues and *Roe* can be judged to concern human rights, the cases are still "twins to be sure" (940).

Indeed, *Roe* appears to be the eviler twin. Ely complains that in *Roe* the Court relies on a "compelling interest" defense, thus requiring a stricter standard for judging the legislative goals than the rational basis test used in the *Lochner* line of cases. In Ely's words, in the *Lochner* cases, the Court said "not that the legislature had incorrectly balanced two legitimate but competing goals, but rather that the goal it had favored was impermissible or the legislation involved did not really promote it" (942). By contrast, in *Roe v. Wade* the Court appears to have substituted its judgment for the legislative balance regarding the relative importance of the goals at stake, making it even more objectionable. Whatever its merits, it is nevertheless difficult for Ely himself to press this critique of *Roe*, because the standard of "strict scrutiny" used to defend compelling interests was developed and used by the Warren Court in decisions Ely staunchly defends. Thus, its role in *Roe v. Wade* cannot serve as the central basis of his objection, at least without further explanation.

In addition, Ely acknowledges that there is a powerful body of opinion that would dismiss this sort of criticism of substantive decision making by the Court as naive. Citing Alexander Bickel,[21] among others, Ely describes their position as follows:

For, the theory goes, except as to the most trivial and least controversial questions (such as the length of a Senator's term), the Constitution speaks in the vaguest and most general terms; the most its clauses can provide are "more or less suitable pegs on which judicial choices are hung." Thus anyone who suggests the Constitution can provide significant guidance for today's difficult questions either deludes himself or seeks to delude the Court. Essentially all the Court *can* do is honor the value preferences it sees fit, and it should be graded according to the judgment and skill with which it does so. (945)

Ely suggests that even many conservatives such as Richard Nixon held this type of view, despite their rhetoric to the contrary. And he points out that academic versions of this position are more subtle and more persuasive than popular versions, in that they urge that justices should not favor their own preferences but rather their best estimate of what over time will be durable values for the American people. Ely appears here to be describing the views of theorists such as Ronald Dworkin, who urges judges to follow values that they believe are embedded in the constitutional history of this country when the Constitution itself fails to give clear guidance,[22] as well as Bickel, Brest, and others mentioned above. After a bit of hand waving at such views, however, Ely rejects them all and concludes that they do not rescue *Roe v. Wade*. In sum, he finds that *Roe* is a very bad decision, not because it will weaken the Court (Ely thinks it will not), and not because it conflicts with Ely's or society's views of social progress (he suggests it does not), but because it is bad constitutional law, or perhaps not even constitutional law at all.

I have already reviewed an outline of what, on Ely's view, makes a decision *good* constitutional law. Ely forthrightly rejects originalism as do most other constitutional law scholars, and he agrees that when there is no wording in the Constitution to help decide a case, the Court often needs something else to rely on. He thus proposes his theory as one that he believes provides a middle ground between strict interpretivism and theories that endorse open-ended external values as legitimate sources of judicial adjudication. What he alludes to in his essay, and defends more fully in his book, is his view that it is legitimate for judges on the Court, when there is no clear guidance in the Constitution's language or the surrounding legislative history, to devote themselves to assuring majority governance while protecting minority rights. His view is a procedural one, which he views as participation oriented and representation reinforcing. Ely's account of justifiable judicial decision making is that the injection of content from some source other than the Constitution is needed, but that this other source must be derived from the general themes of the entire document. His proposal meets these criteria, he believes, while others do not. As he explains it,

The Constitution has . . . proceeded from the quite sensible assumption that an effective majority will not inordinately threaten its own rights, and has sought to assure that such a majority not systematically treat others less well than it treats itself—by structuring decision processes at all levels to try to ensure, first, that everyone's interests will be actually or virtually represented (usually both) at the point of substantive decision, and second, that the processes of individual application will not be manipulated so as to reintroduce in practice the sort of discrimination that is impermissible in theory.[23]

Given this explication of Ely's broader theory of adjudication, it seems to me very clear that Ely's fundamental criticism of *Roe v. Wade* is that it does not follow a defensible constitutional theory. It would be acceptable, on Ely's view, like "activist" Warren Court decisions, if it could be justified according to Ely's own theory encompassing representational goals of the Constitution. But, as I have already shown, Ely believes that application of his theory to the *Roe* case demonstrates that the appropriate outcome would be to defend the less represented minority, namely fetuses, and not mothers.

There are of course a number of ways that one could reply to

Ely. One might reject his theory in its entirety, defending instead Bickel's, Dworkin's, Fuller's, or some other account of constitutional decision making. Alternatively, one could simply accept Ely's critique entirely. I am inclined toward a third option, however, because I have sympathy for Ely's constitutional theory. It seems one could accept his theory of decision making but argue—perhaps even more persuasively—that fetuses, even if they aren't *nothing*, are still not the sort of beings properly viewed as part of the populace to be represented either as a majority or minority. It is certainly arguable that fetuses, even if they can suffer harm at some points in time, are not the sort of minorities to which the framers of the Constitution intended to guarantee protection, or the sort of minorities that, even with adequate representation, could gain and make use of political status or power. Ely repeatedly states that it is irrelevant whether one views a fetus as a person with constitutional rights. However, that claim may undermine this portion of his argument. Ely's own illustration can be used against him (obviously rather tastelessly): dogs (like fetuses) may be able to feel harm, but they are not in virtue of that deserving of political representation as a discrete and insular minority. Moreover, debates over the status of fetal life may reappear as important, contrary to Ely's assertion, in evaluating the extent of harm involved. Even if there is in *Roe* an issue of harm for some or many cases, harm sensed by the fetus may vary over the term of the pregnancy and may not be relevant at the earliest stages of development.[24]

My central claim in this chapter is that if we understand Ely's argument in terms of his own judicial philosophy then it is clear that *none* of these responses entails denying a woman's interest or claim to privacy in the abortion context. To the contrary, Ely's critique is most illuminating if we see it as a *highlighting* the tension between mothers' and fetuses' interests, which we can understand and describe as a conflict between the mother's privacy claim and concerns over harm to the fetus and the fetus's potential for life.

If this is correct, then some will argue that the mother's interest, even if it is a claim to privacy understood inclusively, can *never* outweigh harm to the fetus and the fetus's right to life. Others will strike the balance differently at different points of fetal development, as the *Roe* Court did, urging that the mother's privacy interest is controlling up to a certain point over any interests of the fetus. Alternatively, Ely can be interpreted as maintaining that the only real interest a fetus has is in not suffering pain, and even this holds only insofar as the fetus is sentient. On this view, the only possible conflict of interest between a woman who wants to abort a pregnancy and her fetus is between her privacy right and the fetus's interest in not suffering, which suggests that a woman has an obligation to seek the most painless abortion method consistent with the protection of her own health, but nothing more than this. Nevertheless, on any of these interpretations, Ely's critique need not lead to the view that privacy is irrelevant in *Roe*. The dispute can be viewed as a disagreement over the stringency of the mothers' and fetuses' rights or claims, where privacy *is* the crucial claim for mothers. Pro-life and pro-choice advocates may never reach consensus on that question of stringency, but they need not disagree that privacy is at stake for the mother.

Elsewhere, I have criticized the Supreme Court's retreat from *Roe* in *Webster v. Reproductive Health Services*, a case upholding, in a 5–4 decision, severe restrictions on abortion that make abortions more difficult and expensive to obtain.[25] I stand by that critique but do not reiterate it here. Rather, I am emphasizing that it is reasonable to view *Roe v. Wade* as a case about a meaningful privacy concern for the mother even though there is no explicit mention of "privacy" in the Constitution. Recognizing her privacy claim is compatible with John Hart Ely's influential criticisms of the case. Ultimately, as Ely's critique has correctly and effectively clarified, the crucial controversy in *Roe v. Wade* is the difficult balance between the conflicting interests. As Justice Douglas forewarned in 1971: "The interests of the mother and the fetus are opposed. On which side should the State throw its weight?"[26]

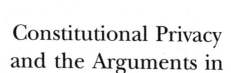

SEVEN

Constitutional Privacy and the Arguments in *Bowers v. Hardwick*

We have seen that constitutional privacy, the most recent right recognized by the Supreme Court, is also one of the most controversial. It has been used to gain powerful protection for individuals, but it has also been criticized as the worst instance of subjective judicial decision making. In this chapter I address another implication of my account of privacy: that is, the extent to which a broad view justifies the legislation of morals. In assessing the majority and minority arguments in the 1986 constitutional privacy case, *Bowers v. Hardwick*, in which the Supreme Court reversed the Eleventh Circuit Court decision and upheld Georgia's anti-sodomy laws,[1] I strongly criticize the decision and its rejection of protection in the name of privacy. The arguments in that case, as well as those from a related debate between Patrick Devlin and H. L. A. Hart, lead to more general conclusions on privacy and the legal enforcement of morality.

It might seem that because *Roe v. Wade* has been the object of such intense dispute, and because the Court refused to allow privacy as a defense for consenting homosexuality in one's home in *Bowers*, the fate of constitutional privacy is sealed as a species soon to be extinct. I argue, to the contrary, that the reasoning in *Bowers* shows the future of privacy may not be so bleak after all and suggests an unexpected positive perspective for the future of constitutional privacy protection. The Court's 5–4 decision in *Bowers v. Hardwick* contains four main sets of arguments and counterarguments; we shall examine each individually.

The Constitutional Question

The first arguments concern the nature and scope of the question at issue in the *Bowers* case. According to Justice White's majority opinion, "The issue presented is whether the Federal Constitution confers a fundamental right upon homosexuals to engage in sodomy and hence invalidates the laws of the many States that still make such conduct illegal and have done so for a very long time" (190). Once the legal question is constructed this narrowly, it is not difficult to see how the majority could defend their view that the clear answer is no. Certainly no right to homosexual sodomy is explicitly mentioned in the Constitution, and at least in the past two hundred years such a right is unlikely to have been endorsed in this country. We have seen in the previous chapter, however, the inadequacies of originalist views of constitutional decision making. The essential issue, then, is whether the majority asked the appropriate constitutional question and whether a moderate theory of judicial adjudication supports the right at stake.

The Georgia law states, in part, "A person commits the offense of sodomy when he performs or submits to any sexual act involving the sex organs of one person and the mouth or anus of another."[2] Atlanta police were pursuing leads on an unrelated charge when they caught Michael Hardwick engaged in a homosexual act in his bedroom. But it is important to note that in the wording of the statute at issue in this case, *no distinction* is made between homosexual and heterosexual behavior, or between married and unmarried partners. Thus it seems the minority is clearly correct in charging that a fair reading of the statute reveals that the majority has distorted the question presented. In addition, to the extent that evidence of any legislative purpose for the 1968 enactment of the statute can be discerned, it seems to have been to *broaden* coverage to reach both homosexual and heterosexual activity, because other laws against homosexuality had been on the books in Georgia for years. Yet the majority never justifies their selective application of the law.

Laurence Tribe encapsulates another way of criticizing the question asked by the Court: "It should come as no surprise that, in the kind of society contemplated by our Constitution, government must offer greater justification to police the bedroom than it must to police the streets. Therefore, the relevant question is not what Michael Hardwick was doing in the privacy of his own bedroom, but what the State of Georgia was doing there."[3]

The Relevance of Privacy

Some commentators have held that "the Supreme Court failed to consider many of the issues Hardwick raised, such as privacy."[4] A careful reading of the decision shows, to the contrary, that the Court did consider the privacy claim, however summarily, and rejected it. Thus the second argument made by the majority is that privacy protection does not extend to the *Bowers* case. They claim that this case has no resemblance to past constitutional privacy cases: "No connection between family, marriage, or procreation on the one hand and homosexual activity on the other has been demonstrated, . . . [and] any claim that these cases nevertheless stand for the proposition that any kind of private sexual conduct between consenting adults is constitutionally insulated from state proscription is unsupportable" (191). This argument goes to the heart of the controversy over what a right to privacy can and should mean. Certainly on narrow and specific grounds it is true that intimate sexual behavior is not the particular issue in any of the previous constitutional privacy cases, although choices about sexual behavior are hardly unrelated to choices about the use of contraceptives. If one thought that constitutional privacy encompasses a broad right to sexual self-determination as a mode of self-expression, then *Bowers* shatters that illusion. More-over, the majority says little to clarify the confusion or to give guidelines for what is covered by privacy.

Nevertheless, privacy was judged to be at stake in protecting the right to choose one's marriage partner and to decide whether to use contraception, to have a child, or even to send one's child to private school. The Court dismisses the relevance of these past constitutional privacy cases by distinguishing them as involving rights related to "family, marriage, or procreation." The minority worries, in contrast, that the Court cites family values as important but chooses to protect only the stereotypical family. They argue, against the majority, that utilitarian concerns as to whether pres-ervation of the family enhances general welfare are irrelevant. By focusing on "marriage, family, and procreation," the majority ig-nores a second dominant theme in past defenses of constitutional privacy: namely, whether a decision or action is fundamental to one's self-identity. The main point is that these rights have in the past been protected because of their importance in the individ-ual's life. They touch central concerns that help define oneself as a person. These minority claims are bolstered by the Court's con-stitutional doctrine that privacy is a "fundamental value" so that state legislation involving privacy deserves a higher level of assess-ment than most other legislation, a standard called "strict scru-tiny."

Moreover, neither access to contraception nor abortion rights are limited to married couples. Indeed, the Court declared in *Eisenstadt v. Baird,* allowing distribution of contraceptives, that dis-tinguishing between married and single persons in such cases is unconstitutional,[5] and the plaintiff in *Roe v. Wade* was unmarried. Hence it is difficult to see how these decisions can be character-ized as focusing on "marriage" and "family." The Court's at-tempt to distinguish *Bowers* from cases concerning procreation may seem on firmer ground. Yet the Court stressed in *Carey v. Population Services International* that the contraception cases protect the decision to engage in sex *without* bearing or begetting a child, applying even to unmarried teenagers.[6] Thus the majority's characterization of previous constitutional privacy cases as focusing on rights related to "family, marriage, and procreation" is unsupportable.

As constitutional scholars have noted, "the Court itself drew an unstable line between some kinds of privacy and others,"[7] giving no reason for the line they drew. They arbitrarily distinguished between traditional intimacies protected in contraception cases and less traditional intimacies with respect to sexual minorities, never even addressing the status of sodomy for heterosexuals. Thus the Court demonstrated that it was willing to protect unenumerated rights in traditional family-oriented contexts, even outside of marriage and for unmarried teenagers, but not similar rights for nontraditional consensual intimate sexuality.[8]

In addition, the Court has repeatedly stated in earlier cases that privacy protects decisions on "fundamental" and "personal" matters, indicating a far closer relationship between the precedents and the *Bowers* case than the majority admits. Previous constitutional privacy cases provide protection of self-expression through the development of close relations with others and protection of control over autonomous decision making in certain contexts. Homosexual acts between consenting adults in one's home provide precisely the sort of context where one is vulnerable to and threatened by scrutiny, pressure to conform, coercion, and exploitation by others, and hence where one needs the shield of privacy. Citing *Paris Adult Theatre I v. Slaton*, the minority scolds, "Only the most willful blindness could obscure the fact that sexual intimacy is 'a sensitive, key relationship of human experience, central to family life, community welfare, and the development of human personality.' "[9]

Even if we acknowledge that the scope of constitutional privacy protection is as yet insufficiently clarified by the Court, if we rely on the Court's own language in previous privacy decisions it is extremely difficult to distinguish *Bowers* from cases where constitutional privacy was upheld. Whatever else might or might not be protected by privacy, Justice Blackmun argues that "the right of an individual to conduct intimate relationships in the intimacy of his or her own home seems to me to be at the heart of the Constitution's protection of privacy" (208). It is interesting to note that philosophers recognize a similar point in contexts unrelated to law. Consider, for example, Stuart Hampshire's remarks: "We know that in the average life nothing is more important in moral consciousness than family and sexual relations, and than love and friendship, and their accepted manners of expression also.... That which is very variable in human relations ... may have profound moral importance."[10] These words aptly summarize expressive privacy as described in chapter 4.

The Slippery Slope Argument

The majority attempts to distinguish *Bowers* from earlier privacy cases on marriage, family, and procreation, while claiming it is *not* differentiable from other cases introduced in its slippery slope argument. The Court could not strike down the Georgia statute and allow consenting homosexual conduct, they argue, while leaving exposed to prosecution adultery, incest, and other sexual crimes, even though the latter are committed within the home. According to the majority opinion, no distinction between homosexual intimacy and incest can be made except by fiat. Sensing danger, they say they are unwilling to travel down that road.

We cannot say that the location of behavior is irrelevant to a privacy decision. The Fourth Amendment protects the "right of the people to be secure in their ... houses," and the view that one's home is one's castle, and governmental interference there is at least prima facie illegitimate, has significance. In addition, the holding in *Stanley v. Georgia*, that obscene matter may be viewed in one's own home, not only rested on a First Amendment argument but was also anchored on respect for the privacy of one's home, since the Court acknowledged that the conduct would not be protected outside the home. *Stanley* even protected behavior not accepted by the majority.[11]

Nevertheless, in *Bowers* the outcome did not, and the majority is correct that it cannot, rest solely on the location of the behavior. We do not condone child abuse or wife battering, in ethics or the law, even if it is done within the confines of the home. And examination of these cases shows clear ground for distinguishing incest and adultery from consensual homosexual relations between adults, namely that incest and (usually) adultery harm someone, as does child abuse and wife battering, while the consensual behavior here at stake does not. The Constitution does not enact John Stuart Mill's harm principle, of course, but harm is clearly a compelling state interest that can override privacy rights.

We may well want to require more justification for governmental intrusion into the home as opposed to other locations. That does not mean, however, that *Bowers* must lead us down the slippery slope feared by the majority. As the Court's reference to other "sexual crimes" indicates, considerations of harm and consent provide important and reasonable ways of making the kind of nonarbitrary distinction the Court claimed was impossible.

The Enforcement of Morals

A final set of arguments focuses not merely on the particulars of this case but on more general issues surrounding morals legislation. In a brief concluding paragraph, Justice White considers the respondent's argument that state legislation must at least pass the rational basis test and that the only basis for the statute is the presumed belief that a majority of the electorate in Georgia find homosexual sodomy to be immoral. White replies for the Court: "The law, however, is constantly based on notions of morality, and if all laws representing essentially moral choices are to be invalidated under the Due Process Clause, the courts will be very busy indeed" (196).

This brief dismissal raises two main concerns. First, it is of course true that the law is infused with morality in many senses. Moral wrongs are often legal wrongs, and moral arguments are made to defend or criticize legislation. Many moral offenses— thefts and murders, for example—are legal offenses. But not every moral wrong is a legal wrong. One is not held liable for every lie or broken promise. Furthermore, saying that the law is "based on" morality does not establish whether or not majority moral views on controversial cases should in every case, or even most cases, be enacted as legislation. It is surely worrisome if White's comment implies that the anti-sodomy law needed nothing more than *some* basis in morality, even a false or dubious majority belief. As some judges have pointed out in gays-in-the-military cases, irrational fear on the part of majorities does not justify discrimination.[12]

Second, White is making a common legal argument about the possible flood of litigation arising from a decision. That some decisions invite more lawsuits, which fill court calendars, is often a major practical concern. Yet *Bowers* does not invite the questioning of *all* moral choices. Legislative statutes are usually justified in a variety of ways. Thus it is unrealistic to believe that the particular facts of the *Bowers* case, had it been decided differently, would have generated a flood of litigation from others believing they had been prosecuted unfairly under laws with no justification beyond the majority moral beliefs of the electorate.

Chief Justice Burger, in his concurring opinion, reiterates the argument for enforcing morality even more strongly: "To hold that the act of homosexual sodomy is somehow protected as a fundamental right would be to cast aside millennia of moral teaching" (197). On one interpretation, Burger is claiming that in light of traditional condemnation of homosexuality, it is hard to claim there is a fundamental right to engage in it. He is perhaps appealing to Justice Frankfurter's traditions of ordered liberty and saying a fundamental right to privacy regarding homosexuality is not in that tradition. But then we might wonder why arguments for a fundamental right encompassing homosexual conduct have to be "traditionalistic" rather than, say, "rationalistic." Indeed, Justice Stevens argues in his dissent that "the fact that the governing majority in a State has traditionally viewed a particular practice as immoral is not a sufficient reason for upholding a law prohibiting the practice; neither history nor tradition could save a law prohibiting miscegenation from constitutional attack" (216).

According to another interpretation, Burger's assumption is that if a moral view is taught or strongly held for a long time, then it is legitimate for the state to codify that moral conviction. Yet the Court's privacy precedents do not uphold this view. Although he found the statute in *Griswold* "uncommonly silly" and "obviously unenforceable," Justice Stewart dissented from the decision to override the doctors' convictions, deferring to the legislature to change the statute. Nevertheless, he cautioned that "it is not the function of this Court to decide cases on the basis of community standards," whatever those standards may be.[13] Philosophers have argued similarly, in general terms totally unrelated to the issue in *Bowers*: "It evidently does not follow from the fact that a way of life has survived, and that it has some hold over men's sentiments and loyalties, that that way of life, with the moral claims which are a necessary element of it, ought for these reasons to be protected and prolonged: there may well be overriding reasons of a rational kind against these claims—that they are unfair or that they destroy happiness."[14] Blackmun's retort for the minority is more scathing: "I cannot agree that either the length of time a majority has held its convictions or the passions with which it defends them can withdraw legislation from this Court's scrutiny" (210).

Arguments for and against the legitimacy of enforcing moral views dominated the debate between Oxford professor of jurisprudence H. L. A. Hart and Patrick Devlin over the 1957 Wolfenden Report to the British government, which recommended legal reform and decriminalization of laws against adult consensual homosexuality and prostitution.[15] Devlin worried that such decriminalization would result in the ultimate moral collapse and destruction of society analogous to that resulting from treason and sedition. Courts must always weigh individual rights to privacy against public security, he agreed, but in cases such as these "immoralities," where the average citizen had not merely a feeling of disgust but disgust "deeply felt and not manufactured," the balance tipped, on Devlin's view, in favor of public welfare.

There are at least two ways of interpreting Devlin's position.[16] First, he might have been urging that the law need not and should not respect John Stuart Mill's harm principle as the only limitation on the state's authority to legislate. In a famous passage in

On Liberty, Mill wrote "that the only purpose for which power can be rightfully exercised over any member of a civilized community, against his will, is to prevent harm to others. His own good, either physical or moral, is not a sufficient warrant."[17] Devlin can be taken as rejecting Mill's view and arguing that even if action causes no harm, it can legitimately be legislated against when there is sufficient public condemnation of the behavior. If this is correct, then Devlin is endorsing a supplement to Mill's harm principle—namely, a principle of moralism, according to which one essential function of the criminal law is to codify and enforce the moral convictions of society.

A second interpretation is that Devlin may have been endorsing a "public" harm principle to justify legislation against these "private immoralities," thereby making the appeal to a principle of moralism unnecessary. The central idea on this reading is that the public is harmed by the knowledge that this behavior is allowed and by the resulting demise of society's morals. Hence society has the right to make such behavior criminal. Devlin's lengthy discussion of public disgust as a test of which moral wrongs can legitimately be legislated against, and the need to take that public feeling seriously in the codification of law, makes the former reading plausible. Yet his focus on the deterioration of society's moral fiber if such behavior is allowed, and his analogies with treason and sedition, make the latter seem to be his more likely emphasis. On this view, Devlin is striking a utilitarian balance, and individual privacy is outweighed by public harm.

Hart countered these arguments in a number of ways. Contrary to Devlin, he endorsed a public/private distinction, arguing that even if certain consensual sexual behavior is judged deviant or immoral, it is nevertheless private behavior not in the appropriate domain of public legislation. The law should not be enforcing private morality where there is no harm to others. Public good, on Hart's view, should be defined in terms of maximization of welfare, not preservation of traditional mores. Moreover, Hart doubted the grave social harm Devlin envisioned, rejected Devlin's inept and unjustified analogies with sedition and treason, and pointed out that the only test Devlin had for determining which "immoralities" should be legislated against was the deep disgust of the average citizen. In part this test reflects an inaccurate picture of society in modern nations whose citizenry displays diverse moral views. Most persuasively, Hart urged that at the very least such strong feelings, even if popular, should be subjected to the most rigorous scrutiny in order to rule out misinformation, misunderstanding, bias, and other prejudice before enacting legislation.

What we learn from Hart's arguments is that it is reasonable to view consensual sexual behavior as private, in the way that a broad construal of privacy endorses, and therefore not a legitimate concern for state criminalization in morals legislation. In such cases forfeiting expressive privacy is too great a cost for securing society's perhaps elusive moral standards. We can also reject Devlin's assumptions that private consensual sexual behavior is harmful and thus a justifiable target for restriction by a Mill-like harm principle. Finally, even if we accept Devlin's view that some "private" behavior can be of legitimate public concern, we can and must reject using as a determinative test whether or not the behavior offends or makes the average person sick. We can recognize the error in using untested or unexamined community morality as the standard for judgment.[18]

Issues raised in this debate are familiar in college philosophy courses and one might think that the Court would take such arguments into account. Hart's concerns about scrutinizing majority moral opinions were not rebutted by Devlin, nor were they anywhere even *mentioned* by the majority of the Court in the *Bowers* case, though they were raised by the minority. Equally telling is the minority's argument that there is a special need to be careful to protect the rights of those who are in a minority, as John Hart Ely has urged.[19] This need is reflected in the Court's past adoption of a policy of tougher scrutiny for legislation that affects a "suspect classification." That constitutional doctrine dictates not merely a rational basis for the statute but more careful scrutiny of the goals of the legislation and the extent to which its means are likely to accomplish those goals, neither of which is addressed by the majority in *Bowers*.

In past cases the Court has enumerated several conditions for determining the existence of a suspect classification. These conditions are that (i) the group must be stigmatized from a history of prejudice,[20] (ii) the class must suffer from unequal treatment,[21] (iii) the classification must be based on some immutable trait that all members share,[22] and (iv) the group must be a discrete and insular minority unable to protect its interests through ordinary political means.[23] Suspect classifications that have been granted this strict scrutiny focus on racial minorities but not women. Sex discrimination cases have to date relied at most on a third tier, "heightened scrutiny."

It is difficult to deny that homosexuals constitute a true minority in numbers as well as being a group that has borne the burden of vehement negative public feelings and discriminatory treatment in public schools, the military, child custody cases, the legal profession, and private employment. Though not part of established law, it is at least arguable on constitutional principles, such as those defended by Ely, that the Court should be especially careful (as they were not) in assessing legislation that affects homosexuals.

The Future of Privacy

My analysis of the arguments in *Bowers* has led to at least four conclusions. First, the majority drew the constitutional question more narrowly than can be defended by the wording of the Georgia statute. Second, they rejected appeals to privacy in a way that is inconsistent with their earlier statements in constitutional privacy cases. Thus the consensual sexual intimacy addressed in *Bowers* can and should be viewed as legitimately private in a broad sense that encompasses expression of self-identity through relationships. Third, the majority argued that a contrary decision in this case would lead down a slippery slope to disaster, allowing crimes such as incest, though there are ample and reasonable grounds to deny any such prospective slide. Finally, they have endorsed arguments on the enforcement of morals almost uniformly rejected by legal theorists and philosophers, without so much as even mentioning those alternative positions or the inconsistency of failing to afford special protection to threatened minorities. Each of these is a serious criticism of the case, and taken together they form a powerful argument that the majority decision in *Bowers* was logically flawed and inadequately justified.

For those directly affected by the case, the consequences of the *Bowers* decision are devastating. It is a worry to all human beings, not only sexual minorities, that all plausible constitutional bases for striking down the anti-sodomy laws were rejected. It is not surprising, therefore, that subsequent cases concerning the discrimination against gays as a class have relied on different arguments, sometimes restricting identification of the respondent as one professing to be gay only, so there is no issue concerning violation of sodomy laws.[24] A more recent national debate has been triggered by a current case in Hawaii, *Baehr v. Miike*, regarding same-sex marriage. In December 1996, Circuit Court Judge Kevin Chang ruled that disallowing same-sex marriage in Hawaii is unconstitutional.[25] The eventual outcome from an appeal to the Hawaii Supreme Court, and from legislation signed by President Clinton in September 1996 barring federal benefits to spouses in same-sex marriages and allowing states to ignore gay and lesbian marriages legalized in other states, will undoubtedly have multiple ramifications for future case law regarding sexual minorities.

"The Court is most vulnerable and comes nearest to illegitimacy when it deals with judge-made constitutional law having little or no cognizable roots in the language or design of the Constitution" (194), announces White in his majority opinion in *Bowers*. He is clearly referring to worries that constitutional privacy was insufficiently defended as a constitutional guarantee when it was announced in *Griswold*. Apparently his argument is that defending Hardwick's rights under constitutional privacy will be equally problematic more than twenty years later. But the twenty years of cases since *Griswold* have provided a powerful set of precedents that, I argued in the previous chapter, an acceptable and nonoriginalist theory of constitutional adjudication cannot ignore.

The majority gives no explanation for narrowing the constitutional question posed in *Bowers* and even appears to go out of its way to restrict the issue, giving the impression of procedural manipulation. Because, in addition, the majority opinion contains a tone of disapproval and language strongly condemning homosexuality, it reads as if the majority made up its mind to deny homosexuals constitutional protection and then applied traditional moral views to defend its position, ignoring the Court's own contrary arguments and the authority of precedent. Sadly, Justice Stevens suggests just that in his conclusion that the majority excludes homosexuals from the Constitution's protection simply because it dislikes them (219).[26]

If *Bowers* rests on nothing but the collective distaste and emotional response of five judges predisposed against Hardwick, then given the precedents on privacy and their links to *Bowers* it is *at least as plausible* to judge the decision in *Bowers* as vulnerable, itself judge-made law approaching illegitimacy. Critics of the Warren Court have shown convincingly that judges *do* abuse their power when they depart from explicit rules and consistency with precedent to achieve a result they find desirable on other grounds. Courts *should* take logic, precedent, and consistency seriously.[27] But as we have seen, it is the majority opinion in *Bowers,* not the minority, that is least well justified constitutionally.

There is a further major concern: that constitutional decision making will change dramatically if the Court continues in other cases to draw the question narrowly as it did in *Bowers.* If the justices do so, they can undermine, restrict, and even retrench many individual rights, not merely privacy. Such a restricted focus is potentially even more threatening to individual rights if it is combined with an originalist view of constitutional decision making, because new technology brings issues the framers of the Constitution did not and could not have foreseen. This is a second sense in which *Bowers* is a particularly troubling decision.

It has been argued, however, that there is a glimmer of hope in the *Bowers* judgment. Because the constitutional question was drawn so narrowly, the majority opinion need not be read to extend to heterosexuals.[28] Consensual sodomy statutes aimed at heterosexuals have been held, and should remain, unconstitutional. Ultimately, Laurence Tribe believes, *Bowers* "does not necessarily doom any and all sexual privacy claims relating to unorthodox or nonmarital sex between consenting adults."[29] This is not to support the *Bowers* decision, but to point out that sexual self-determination is not totally jettisoned by the Court and to acknowledge that protecting the privacy interests of some is better than protecting none at all. Indeed, it would be preferable to enforce the statute as written, making no distinction between heterosexual and homosexual behavior, because that would force a greater degree of political responsibility on the legislature. Legislators would then have to face the majority whose rights also have been restricted. Another view is that *Bowers* can be read as drawing the far boundary of the privacy right in sexual matters.[30] That interpretation may be correct, even if the wrong boundary was drawn. The Court refused to expand privacy protection and may continue to resist further expansion in other areas.

Nevertheless, it does not follow that *Bowers* significantly narrows the scope of privacy rights, as some commentators have suggested.[31] Taking that view obscures an ironically positive side to the decision. Given (i) that *Bowers* was decided on such narrow grounds, solely on the question whether or not there is a constitutional right to homosexual sodomy; (ii) that privacy was deemed irrelevant to the case; and (iii) that the case was ardently distinguished from previous constitutional privacy cases, then the judgment does not pose the threat to constitutional privacy that it might have. I have argued that the Court erred seriously in its decision. Nevertheless, privacy may profit from the error. Having announced that *Bowers* has no link to previous privacy cases, the Court cannot use it consistently and rationally to overturn those privacy rights.

EIGHT

Drug Testing:
A Case Study in Balancing
Privacy and Public Safety

Recent increases in the use of illegal drugs and problems related to that use have raised a variety of public health and safety concerns and have led many to propose drug testing as one of the best ways to combat the proliferation of drug use. Similar calls for increased testing have arisen because of the spread of the human immunodeficiency virus (HIV) and the threat it poses to those exposed to it.[1] Clearly, these public health and safety concerns conflict with multiple privacy claims of those being targeted for testing. Nevertheless, many view the public safety threat as serious enough to completely override any individual privacy interests. Indeed, public opinion polls indicate that there is widespread support for a variety of testing programs, even those that are random and mandatory.[2]

Drug testing is a particularly useful issue to address in this book because the diverse privacy claims it raises encompass and link the full range of tort, Fourth Amendment, and other constitutional privacy concerns I have discussed. But it is misleading to view a public policy decision about when and how to conduct drug tests as a simple choice between privacy and public safety.

The issues surrounding testing programs are far more complex than the foregoing suggests, even if that complexity is often ignored. It is both difficult and unwise to reach conclusions about whether testing programs are justified without specifying what type of testing is being proposed (e.g., blood, urine), what is being tested for (e.g., alcohol, drugs, HIV infection), who is initiating the tests (e.g., government agencies, employers, insurance companies), the goals of the tests and the likelihood that they will reduce or eradicate the problem, the harm that would result without the tests, the costs of the proposed testing program, the accuracy of the type of test under consideration, whether confirmatory tests will be added, whether the testing will be mandatory or voluntary, whether the tests will be random or will selectively target particular groups, whether an identifiable showing of suspicion or performance decline will prompt the tests, and how test results will be used and distributed. Furthermore, one must assess which goals of a particular drug-testing program are achievable and must balance those against the consequences of the testing. The crucial question is to determine when that balance provides adequate moral justification for the testing: that is, when the privacy claims are determinative and when they may be legitimately overridden.

It should be clear from the above list of concerns that drug testing illustrates both the complexity of contemporary privacy debates and the difficulty of making broad generalizations. Nevertheless, drug testing serves well as a case study showing how to reach justified conclusions using the strategy I proposed in chapter 4. The controversy over drug testing illustrates the importance of beginning with a presumption in favor of privacy and then showing how to justify a balance between privacy and conflicting values. Major public health and safety goals can be addressed seriously while still taking precautions to protect privacy vigorously. Drug abuse should not be tolerated in the workplace or elsewhere that it threatens the safety of others. But care must be taken to limit the extent to which drug testing intrudes on people's privacy. The ideal is to use the technology selectively, with adequate moral justification, and with enough safeguards and precautions to ensure that the testing is done thoughtfully and responsibly.

Arguments in Favor of Drug Testing

Both the government and private employers argue that they have a significant interest in testing citizens and employees for a wide variety of reasons: to fight the "drug war" by weeding out users and curbing drug use, to ensure safety by revealing conditions that pose a serious threat to coworkers or the public, to maintain an unimpaired and effective workforce, to identify those who will be unable to work in the future, to reduce the costs of employee health care plans, and to maintain public confidence in the integrity and trustworthiness of their operations. Insurers argue in addition that testing is necessary because it is fundamentally unfair to require relatively healthy policyholders to subsidize the costs of health care and life insurance benefits for those with high mortality risks; they also insist that banning insurer testing might leave the industry financially unable to afford to offer individual insurance policies at all.[3] Taken together, these provide strong political, moral, and economic reasons to take seriously the option of drug testing in some form.

Moreover, the alarming levels of drug abuse in America are estimated to be very costly. The illegal narcotics traffic of about $27 billion to $110 billion each year correlates with the rising crime rate. In fact, studies showing that "drug use is very much a characteristic of serious and violent offenders" and that "increasing or reducing the level of drug abuse is associated with a corresponding increase or reduction in criminality" may have provided the earliest theoretical justification for initiating drug testing programs.[4] A further consequence is increased medical expenses and rehabilitation costs for drug users. It has also been claimed that the industrial costs of drug abuse are enormous. As one commentator on drug testing explains, "In human terms they include lost jobs, injuries, illnesses, and deaths. In economic terms they include property damage, tardiness, absenteeism, lost productivity, quality control problems, increased health insurance costs, increased worker's compensation costs, the cost of replacing and training new employees, and employee theft."[5] According to government estimates, drug abuse cost employers in the United States $33 billion in 1985. More recently, government officials have claimed that these costs are as high as $60 to $100 billion.[6]

Drug testing is taken seriously as a partial solution to the growing drug problem because of the purported results of urinalysis programs instituted by many agencies and employers. Private companies report that the effects of drug-testing programs include increased employee productivity, enhanced job efficiency, significant declines in lost work time and accident rates, and decreased risk to other employees and the public. If correct, these findings suggest that employer-initiated testing is an efficient way of addressing employee drug abuse and may be a useful deterrent in other contexts as well.

Indeed, drug testing is now commonplace for many workers. In 1986 President Reagan authorized the testing of all federal job applicants and ordered random testing of federal employees in positions referred to as "safety-sensitive." Mandatory preemployment screening for job applicants and sometimes random urinalysis of current employees are utilized at numerous private businesses, including IBM, DuPont, Exxon, Lockheed, FedEx, AT&T, the *New York Times*, some Wall Street firms, and over 25 percent of Fortune 500 companies.[7] Testing for truck drivers and rapid transit and airline workers is mandated by federal law; testing of law enforcement officials and athletes is also widespread.[8] And recent court cases continue to address the constitutionality of testing teachers, postal workers, customs officials, criminal suspects, prisoners, and many others. The tests are so pervasive that according to the National Institute on Drug Abuse (NIDA) as many as 15 million working Americans had their urine tested for illegal drugs in 1990.[9] Interestingly, these high numbers increase the amounts of money involved, and so have further complicated the issue by making drug testing a very profitable business.

Threats to Privacy

Despite its popularity, there is good reason to question the justifiability of drug testing. Supreme Court Justice Antonin Scalia, for example, has referred to the practice as a "needless indignity." Drug testing clearly intrudes on individual privacy in a number of distinct ways. One central concern is the technological and physical intrusiveness into a person's body and biological functions in the actual procedures used for collecting samples. If a blood test is used, it necessarily involves puncturing the skin. If a urinalysis is required, the sample must sometimes be gained under direct observation to guard against drug-free substitutions and falsification of results. The additional physical and psychological intrusion of urinating on demand, under surveillance, is far from minimal. Compare, for example, similar privacy issues concerning bodily integrity raised in early influential and foundational privacy cases such as *DeMay v. Roberts*, discussed in chapter 1, and in *Union Pacific Railway v. Botsford*, described in chapter 4. Critics of testing also point out that there are less intrusive ways to identify drug abusers, mainly stressing observation to detect impairment. Clearly drug tests threaten accessibility privacy by giving others unwanted observational and physical access to oneself.

Moreover, besides confirming or disconfirming the presence of drugs in the body, analysis of blood and urine samples may reveal numerous physiological facts about the party being tested that he or she may not want shared with others, and thus such analyses threaten informational privacy as well. Tests can reveal information about such conditions as contraceptive use, pregnancy, epilepsy, manic depression, diabetes, schizophrenia, and heart trouble. Revelations of this sort are particularly troubling because they raise multiple privacy questions concerning acquisition, storage, use, and distribution of the information. Consider, for example, how the results of drug tests are handled. In some testing programs, individuals are not even notified that their samples will be tested. If they are notified and then are informed of the results, it is usually not clear who else has access to the results and what controls there are for maintaining the confidentiality of the information the test reveals. Disclosure of information from drug tests can be not only embarrassing but can lead to discrimination, loss of employment, and financial loss. There is a serious worry that the individual has absolutely no control over any information gained from the tests.

Another argument against testing is that it is reasonable to maintain that employees should be free from scrutiny of their activities during their nonworking hours as long as their activities are not affecting their performance. Hence drug testing also threatens expressive privacy by intruding on one's body and behavior, making one fearful about one's choice of activities. An evaluation of drug-testing programs clearly involves attending to all the privacy issues addressed in this book—control over information about oneself, Fourth Amendment searches, and constitutional concerns about intrusions into and control over one's body and decisions—underscoring how intertwined these various privacy claims can be.

Further Arguments against Testing: Accuracy Concerns

Opponents of drug testing also focus on the limitations of the testing procedures, arguing that the tests are highly inaccurate. Assessing concerns about test accuracy is crucial because inaccuracy exacerbates threats to privacy. It may well be that it is necessary to have far more vigilance and control over the information gathered from the tests, and place more weight on requiring privacy protection, when there is a high probability that the information is mistaken.

One worry about accuracy is the sensitivity of the tests. Many types of tests, opponents argue, yield inaccurate results as often as 60 percent of the time. Even if the tests are more highly accurate, they claim, innocent parties will be harmed because most tests produce a large number of false positives, results indicating drug use when there has been none. Such false positives can arise from the use of medications or from such accidents as passive inhalation of marijuana smoke. Critics worry, moreover, that the laboratories evaluating the tests also create errors, caused both by the limitations of technology and by human error.

A related issue involves the problems of interpreting the results of drug tests. Most tests set a threshold level above which the result is deemed to establish drug use. But there are few standards for determining how or where that level should be set. Moreover, a true positive may indicate an isolated incident of drug use, not a habitual pattern; interpretation of results does not usually differentiate the two or reveal when the drug was used.

Another serious concern is that the tests cannot establish whether a subject is under the influence of a drug at the time the test is administered, and the tests are incapable of determining if and how much drug use impairs the individual's performance level or actually affects his or her behavior. There is general agreement in the scientific community that "testing does not discriminate between drug use that impairs performance and drug use that does not impair performance. It does not even determine impairment at the time of the test."[10] At best, what is established is whether a person's body contains traces of chemicals that may indicate previous use. Short of this, tests may merely indicate involuntary exposure or an error in procedure. Thus the test results may show only conditions, not performance related, that are not relevant for determining employment or the quality of performance. Even the tests that appear not to be arbitrary are problematic.

Critics also worry that tests justified for people in safety-sensitive positions can be abused because of the malleability of the term "safety-sensitive." Legislators or employers may expand the definition so that it becomes a camouflage for unprincipled random testing.

The most commonly administered drug tests are conducted through urinalysis, in part because these are less intrusive than blood tests and in part because they are less expensive to administer. Urinalyses can be divided into two types. The most frequently used are administered as presumptive screening tests. The most common involves the enzyme multiplied immunoassay technique (EMIT); others are the radioimmunoassay (RIA) and the thin layer chromatography (TLC) tests. These tests are intended to easily, rapidly, and inexpensively identify specimens that most likely contain the sought-after substances. One limit of immuno-assay tests is that they are designed to detect only one drug or metabolite or a few closely related ones. The (sometimes erro-neous) assumption is that a positive test identifies a user—of ma-rijuana, cocaine, or amphetamines, for example—and a negative test shows a nonuser. Although relatively inexpensive, the screen-ing tests are recognized to be nonspecific and insensitive.[11] In those programs that add confirmatory tests, a second and more accurate procedure, gas chromotography-mass spectrometry (GC/MS) assessment, is also used. In these cases, a sample is reported positive only if both the screening and confirmatory tests are pos-itive. But these tests are complex, slow to complete, and more expensive than immunoassay tests. A single GC/MS test costs $75 or more. And it is worth noting that confirmatory tests for some drugs are not readily available.

The reliability of the immunoassay screening test is under-mined by many factors, alluded to above. The high rate of false positives cited by critics can arise from temperature changes in the sample or the presence of substances other than the ones being sought. Positive cannabinoid results have been obtained from urine samples of people who have taken anti-inflammatory drugs such as ibuprofen (Advil, Motrin, and so on) or naproxen, and similar medications might affect the results of tests for bar-biturates. Cold remedies such as Contac or Sudafed can suggest the presence of amphetamines, and positive tests for morphine can be obtained from those who have taken drugs containing codeine, including many popular cough syrups. A metabolite of cocaine was measured in a subject who had had one cup of an herbal tea that was alleged to have contained decocainized coca leaves, but in fact had about 5 mg of cocaine per tea bag.[12]

Thus, critics conclude,

a positive urine test, regardless of the absolute concentration of the sam-ple, provides no information on the amount of drug ingested or inhaled, the time or duration of exposure, or the behavioral effect of the drug. A positive test, if confirmed, may establish exposure, but it does not confirm drug abuse or intoxication, either at the time the sample was obtained or any time prior to that; conversely, a negative test does not rule out abuse or intoxication.[13]

The frequency of false positive and negative test results indicates the importance of conducting confirmatory tests on samples. But the cost and time required limit the extent to which such follow-up tests are used. Moreover, even a combination of screening and confirmatory tests is susceptible to glaring deficiencies. The threshold or cutoff value that separates positive and negative test results varies depending on the amount of the drug being tested for. If the cutoff is set too low, then a confirmatory test may not actually confirm the result of the initial screening test. If the cutoff is set too high, some positive specimens may be missed, but the rate of confirmations will be higher. As one critic of drug testing observes, "Decisions on choosing cutoffs depend on how many false negatives, false positives, and unconfirmed test results are economically and scientifically acceptable."[14] When donors are being tested for blood banks, allowing more false positives is clearly preferable to allowing any false negatives. But in other contexts the balance is less clear, and value judgments may differ more widely.

Another difficulty is that those with sufficient will can find ways to defeat the tests. Those who practice timed abstinence or who ingest large amounts of fluid can dilute the concentration of a drug in urine to below the cutoff amount. Adding salt, vinegar, bleach, liquid soap, blood, or another foreign substance can adulterate samples and produce false negative results that hide possible abuse. Preventing adulteration of samples may lead to testing protocols that require direct observation of specimen collections.[15]

Quality control in the lab also calls into question the accuracy of test results. Critics claim that technicians are often given minimal training. Procedural mishaps as simple as misidentifying a sample may occur; moreover, unskilled technicians may not know how to interpret the findings. Signs of a single instance of marijuana use, for example, can persist in urine samples for days or even weeks, but lab workers might not recognize the importance of including such information along with a positive result. Private laboratories claim that their work is 95 to 99 percent accurate, but they have given little documentation for their claims, nor have the results of testing of the labs' proficiency been made available.[16]

To the extent that drug tests produce false negatives, they are ineffective in identifying users. For those who test positive falsely, privacy respecting control over the information is paramount, as the implications for their reputation, employment, and freedom may be grave indeed. It is widely agreed that blood tests are more accurate than urinalysis in gauging the evidence of intoxication or abuse of alcohol and other drugs. Because concentrations in the blood are usually proportional to concentrations in the brain, blood tests are also likely to measure performance capacity more reliably. In addition, blood tests are taken directly from individuals by lab personnel, so tampering with specimens is almost impossible when the technicians are trustworthy. But analyses of blood specimens are also more difficult, complex, and costly. Moreover, because blood concentrations peak and decrease very rapidly, and back calculations in time are rarely possible for most drugs, there is often just a short window of time when a blood test will be useful.

Reviewing the Threat to Public Safety

Given the many difficulties associated with the implementation and accuracy of drug tests, and the numerous and serious ways in which the privacy of subjects can be compromised, it is worth reexamining the evidence that urine tests, even with confirmatory testing, will result in improvement in health, safety, and performance. While such claims are made regularly, it is difficult to find data to back them up. It is also difficult to assess the extent to which drug-testing programs have a deterrent effect. Many in the medical field argue bluntly that "objective biomedical science tells us that urine testing is of no value in coping with illicit drug use."[17]

Even regarding transportation accidents, where drug impairment is claimed to play a statistically large role, evaluations of the evidence are unclear. After nearly every plane or rail crash there is (often sensational) publicity about drug tests for pilots and engineers. It is rare, however, for the data to show that employees were impaired by drugs other than alcohol, or that random urine drug testing would have prevented the accident. One critic has pointed out that "for testing to be fully effective, every worker would have to be tested daily for every drug that might impair performance, the results would have to be available before he started work, and he would have to be under constant surveillance while at work to make sure he did not use a drug while working."[18]

It is worth noting that marijuana accounts for a huge majority of positive findings nationwide—perhaps as many as 90 percent—because it is the most widely used illegal drug and because it persists in urine for a month or more, compared to two days for most drugs. Yet because of its persistence, many of those true positive drug tests have little or no implication for the worker's actual performance. Finally, it is unclear that the threat of drug use is increasing, as proponents of testing insist. A 1989 NIDA report contradicted claims of increasing illegal drug use. According to the report, illegal drug use has been decreasing for ten years, and the decline accelerated over the latter five of those years.[19]

Thus the correlation between drug use and unsafe job performance is not definitely established. Nevertheless, there are studies that show a significant correlation between positive drug tests and poorer scores on certain general measures of job performance, such as absenteeism and dismissal for other reasons. In addition, studies of airline pilots under simulated conditions indicate diminished ability to perform various maneuvers when there has been prior drug use, including marijuana. Thus there is at least some evidence of a correlation between drug use and performance, particularly in one safety-sensitive occupation, suggesting a possible role for appropriately targeted drug tests. One challenge, then, is to determine when drug testing will actually contribute to the goals of public health and safety sufficiently to override the privacy intrusions of testing.

Constitutional Guidelines and the Courts

The first two cases on drug testing to reach the Supreme Court were argued in 1988. In the decisions, issued the following year, the Court clearly held that urine tests are a significant intrusion into a fundamentally private domain.[20] Since then, virtually every court that has addressed the issue has found that urinalysis and blood tests intrude on privacy as a search and seizure under the Fourth Amendment. Courts have mainly focused on the privacy invasions involved first in the process of urination and the manner in which the specimen is obtained and, second, in the individual's interest in safeguarding the confidentiality of the information contained in the sample. Courts routinely acknowledge that drug tests also violate the Fifth Amendment guarantee against self-incrimination, the Fourteenth Amendment protection of due process, and constitutional privacy interests protecting choice and bodily integrity. However, many courts have taken the privacy claims of the Fourth Amendment to be either the most forceful or the most easily defensible constitutional threats. Courts have been somewhat divided over how intrusive unobserved urinalysis testing is. But they have generally agreed that compulsory urinalysis infringes on an individual's expectation of privacy both in the process and in the loss of control over information. Nevertheless, case law currently indicates that some drug screening is constitutionally permissible. Fourth Amendment protection is not absolute, and the courts have traditionally used a two-part test to decide when the government has infringed an individual's Fourth Amendment privacy. First, the individual must show a "subjective expectation of privacy," and second, the expectation must be "one that society considers reasonable."[21]

The key, then, is the determination of when drug tests are "reasonable." No court has held testing to be a violation of the

Fourth Amendment when there is a showing of "reasonable suspicion" that the individual has been using illegal drugs. But the Supreme Court also allowed the testing of any customs officials in positions that directly involve the interdiction of drugs or that require firearms to be carried in the line of duty. The evolving legal standard is that reasonable suspicion be required except for random testing upheld for public employees who hold safety-sensitive positions, work in law enforcement positions, or have access to classified materials. The Supreme Court most recently addressed the "reasonableness" of the expectation of privacy in 1995, upholding a random urinalysis program for student athletes. In assessing the legitimacy of the privacy expectation, the Court noted the evidence of drug use by athletes but focused on the fact that the program was aimed at public school students in grades 7 to 12 under supervision and temporary custody of the state, making the decision less remarkable than it might otherwise have been.[22]

It is not surprising that courts have taken Fourth Amendment privacy seriously in the context of drug tests. As discussed in chapter 1, stomach pumping, strip searches, and body cavity checks to gain evidence have historically been judged unconstitutional. By analogy, although United States banks are surely concerned to ensure that their employees are not embezzlers, that worry does not entitle them to search all bank employees and their homes on the chance that they may uncover a dishonest employee.[23]

It is troubling, however, that many courts have refused to address the issue of testing error, have avoided discussions of the implications of false positives and false negatives, and have underemphasized the physical bodily intrusion related to constitutional privacy concerns surrounding control over one's body, as well as worries about social control over behavior off the job. Moreover, protection against warrantless and unreasonable searches does not apply in the private sector, and most private-sector drug-testing programs have survived legal challenge thus far. State regulations are largely absent. The few that have been enacted form a patchwork of conflicting guidelines.[24] Some, such as Utah's, promote employer interests by allowing random testing of all employees. Others have been more sensitive to employee interests, but the great majority of states have no guidelines at all. Still, the model of the courts embracing a basic concern with protecting Fourth Amendment privacy may indicate that those companies initiating testing programs that do not take sufficient care to address privacy intrusions will face an increasing risk of liability.

Privacy in the Balance: Ethical Justifications

Certainly there is a very real problem of drug abuse in this country. Yet drug testing in the workplace may not be the most effective way of tackling the problem. As we have seen, there is good reason to worry that privacy is not protected strenuously enough and that drug tests cannot adequately protect others from harm as intended. The considerations discussed above provide compelling arguments that widespread and random drug testing is unnecessarily intrusive, unwise, and inefficient. It might seem, therefore, that we have reached the inevitable conclusion that drug testing is never morally justifiable.[25] But such a conclusion would be too hasty. That a practice is difficult to justify does not make it impossible to justify in all cases: a presumption favoring privacy is not a trump. The key moral issues involve determining when the interests of others are significant enough to outweigh the privacy threats to test subjects and when the achievable goals outweigh the negative consequences of testing. Although I cannot address every conceivable case, I believe that in carefully circum-scribed circumstances, drug testing can be defended as morally justifiable, overriding a presumption in favor of privacy. But such testing must be administered with stringent procedural safeguards designed to help protect privacy.

Some cases appear uncontroversial. It seems clear that tests should be permissible and perhaps even mandated for potential blood donors, for several reasons. The expectation is that donated blood will be clean, and the interests of those needing transfu-sions are highly significant. The consequences of tainted blood are often life-threatening, and the risk of harm to the recipient is immediate and certain. Such testing is not random, moreover, but targets only those wishing to donate blood, and the results of such tests performed by organizations like the Red Cross are confidential.

In less clear cases, the practice can be justified only if there is a substantial and demonstrable likelihood that a significant drug problem exists, and if the testing program targets those potentially causing the problem with evidence that it can be alleviated. That is, the presumption in favor of privacy shows the privacy intrusions enumerated above are significant enough to require *substantial evidence* of an existing drug problem and a *reasonable expectation* of resolving it, before testing becomes morally justifiable. If there is probable cause or reasonable suspicion to believe there is a drug use problem, such as substantial evidence of frequent use or abuse of drugs by a group or individual over a significant amount of time, and if it can be shown likely to be affecting the safety of customers (e.g., passengers), coworkers, or products, then random testing and follow-up to single out those risking the welfare of others gains ethical force over a presumption of privacy. Thus I support, for instance, the Supreme Court's decision in *Skinner v. Railway Labor Executives' Association* to allow tests of railway workers where there was evidence of frequent alcohol and drug use and a demonstrated connection between use and accidents. In that particular case it appeared that the safety threat was clear, it was substantial (at least 23 percent of the railway workers were found to be "problem drinkers"), and the subjects formed a targeted group that, if it became drug-free, could decrease the railway accident rate substantially.

Additionally, when individuals or groups show some evidence of performance impairment and the likelihood of a serious accident or defective product is thereby significantly heightened by it, drug testing may also be morally justified. Even if it is not certain that the impairment is due to drug use, the individual's behavior can be worrisome enough to defeat claims that he or she must not be intruded upon. The presumption of a person's innocence is, in such cases, rightly called into question. A drug test, administered with procedural safeguards, can help determine if drug use is indeed contributing to the poor performance observed. In sum, neither claims to privacy nor studies concerning difficulties with drug tests rule out testing when some substantial causal showing, performance impairment, or reasonable suspicion of drug use exists.

But absent such evidence, drug-testing programs instituted to accomplish general deterrence of drug use, or based on generalized claims about the need to fight the "war on drugs," do not carry sufficient moral justification to outweigh all the negative consequences and difficulties of drug testing. With no showing of a significant problem, there is too little evidence that any deterrent effect or any progress in combating drug use will result. Thus I find insufficient ethical justification for the Supreme Court's judgment in *National Treasury Employees v. Von Raab*, which upheld random testing of customs workers by virtue of the job they held, even though there was almost no evidence of a drug problem either by individuals or across a section of the group of customs workers. No adequate justification was given for the privacy intrusion.[26]

One difficulty of mandating testing for persons in positions that count as safety-sensitive is in ensuring that "safety-sensitive" is an accurate, not merely expedient, classification. Moreover, people holding positions where they are required to carry firearms or have access to classified material have already been subjected to extensive background checks. The Court in *Von Raab* appealed to a generalized compelling interest that customs employees not use drugs even when off duty and to the extraordinary safety and national security hazards of drug use among customs officials. But when taken with the admission that customs is largely drug-free and that previous drug use was not the reason for establishing the testing program, those appeals lose moral force. The actual purposes cited for the testing were to deter drug use among employees in the specified positions and to keep drug users from being promoted into such positions. It was claimed that customs officials who use drugs are more susceptible to bribery and that those in jobs where they may use firearms depend uniquely on their judgment and dexterity, both of which could be compromised by drug use. Yet there was at most a potential for harm to others, but no clear threat of harm. Furthermore, there was virtually no evidence that any customs officials had a drug problem and so no reason to suppose that there was any need to deter any of them, or that testing could reduce drug use. There was thus little likelihood the testing program would have any impact at all.

I have argued that several criteria must be met for drug-testing programs to be deemed morally justifiable. The most basic is that a significant drug problem must actually be apparent, whether through a causal showing, performance impairment, or other reasonable source of suspicion. We might well consider, therefore, whether a less objectionable alternative, focusing more directly on performance, can effectively protect the public from harm. Some have argued, for example, that state-of-the-art employee assistance programs, combined with proper education of supervisory personnel, can be as effective or more effective than drug testing in minimizing harm to others.[27]

This is a provocative suggestion, and it may be that when fully developed, such programs ultimately will be able to supersede drug testing even in the cases where I have defended it. At present, however, there are a number of difficulties with advocating such programs in place of all drug testing. First, the educational process of supervisors is critical, and adequate development and implementation could be very time-consuming. It would be a mistake to underestimate how extensively personnel must be educated for such programs to be successful. Second, employee assistance programs could be more costly and thus less feasible economically than drug-testing programs. Small businesses, for example, may find it prohibitively expensive to introduce adequate employee assistance programs for only a few isolated cases. Third, it is difficult to see how to mandate procedural safeguards for employees when the programs are individualized and run by supervisory personnel. Some may worry about what recourse or appeal mechanism an employee has if a supervisor is distrustful or is erroneously convinced of an employee's abuse. Drug-testing programs have the virtue, perhaps, of being more easily subject to federal regulations that uniformly protect test subjects' interests.

Ideally and more characteristically, however, employee assistance programs are set up so supervisory personnel only refer employees to health care professionals for assessment and treatment recommendations. These assistance programs are not intended to determine wrongdoing. Rather, their goal is to provide help for employees who need it, with the assurance of continued employment if treatment is successful. Perhaps the most notable difficulty with these programs is the lack of hard evidence that a high percentage of employees with chemical dependencies are actually identified and then treated.

Procedural Safeguards and Recommendations

The presumption in favor of recognizing the multiple threats to informational, accessibility, and expressive privacy in drug testing remains strong. Therefore even in the narrowly circumscribed cases when drug testing can be ethically justified on my view, I believe it is necessary to mandate precautions to protect privacy and minimize error. To be effective, these should be federal guidelines that are backed up with sanctions for violations and that recommend combining test results with follow-up assessments of performance.

To reiterate, we should mandate that drug tests be conducted only after evidence suggests a reasonable probability of drug abuse. Reasonable suspicion might be indicated if there is perceived impairment, deficient output or performance, a major unexplained change in attitude, or other behavior arousing suspicion. When reasonable suspicion is required before testing, the intrusion into workers' privacy is better justified, the testing program is less vulnerable to constitutional attack, and supervisors are forced to oversee more rigorously the performance of those in their charge.[28]

Even when fully justified, drug-testing plans should be explained in writing, and those who might be tested should be made

aware of the reasons for th⸱   ⸱ng program. They will then know
whether the testing w⸱⸱   ⸱ect observation, whether it will
be voluntary or ⸱⸱   ⸱ition of employment, and so
on. We migh⸱   ⸱oyees be informed in advance
whether a \   e random or required as a condition c   \   ⸱e of the inadequacies and inaccuracies o⸱ \   ⸱ests, we should require that whoever
initiates a te⸱   \   ⸱ give confirmatory tests for those with
positive results   ⸱ual screening is selective, as I have argued
it should be, the ⸱ ⸱ of confirmatory testing will not be prohib-
itive. People testing positive should be allowed an opportunity to
explain the test results and to have the sample retested at an
independent laboratory.

We can hope that the testing technology being developed by
Roche, Abbott, and other companies will continue to improve.
Methods are being discovered to discern from a test if a common
medication has been the cause of a false positive result. The possibility of less intrusive and more accurate tests—using saliva or
hair samples, for example—is also under investigation. In the
meantime, it seems reasonable to require laboratories to justify
the thresholds used for determining positive and negative read-
ings on tests. Laboratories ought also to be required to state the
length of time a given drug remains in the system, the test's ina-
bility to determine performance limitations, and similar relevant
information. By setting the results in perspective, this will help
explain what they mean. It might also be reasonable to mandate
laboratory procedures such as documenting all handling of a sample and dividing all samples, one part to be analyzed and one as
a backup to be frozen, in case the results are contested later.

Finally, detailed guidelines must be set up to protect the confidentiality of the information gained from tests. The growth of
computer databases of medical information may make it almost
impossible to guarantee confidentiality. But it can certainly be a
legal requirement, with strong sanctions for noncompliance, that
test results not be used for any purpose other than that originally
articulated, and that test information not be released without per-

mission to anyone other than the individual tested. Confidentiality can be further enhanced by requiring "anonymous" testing, which marks samples by coded numbers rather than names.

This may appear to be a burdensome list of requirements to impose on testing programs. But the requirements not only protect individual privacy, they also encourage government and employers to use testing only when it is most likely to be helpful in averting public harm. Time, energy, and money not used on widespread random tests could then be better spent on monitoring performance through observation, controlling alcohol abuse on the job, and limiting illegal drug traffic in the United States.

My goal has been to strike a balance between the very real and numerous privacy intrusions involved in drug testing and the need to protect public safety when drug abuse is a substantial threat. It is important to recognize the benefits of drug testing when there is probable cause or clear substantial evidence of abuse, with likely correlation to a safety threat and a reasonable possibility of achieving the desired effects. Conversely, mass testing without suspicion is intrusive, inefficient, often inaccurate, and a waste of resources. Furthermore, even when tests are morally justifiable in spite of a strong presumption of privacy, they should be conducted subject to strict regulations aimed at maximizing privacy and accuracy of results, while still allowing the identification of those who use illegal drugs.

NINE

Information Technology:
A Challenge to Privacy Protection

As technological advances continue, individual privacy is threatened more consistently and more pervasively. Developing information technologies renew concerns about "core" privacy interests addressed in tort and Fourth Amendment law, described in chapter 4 under "informational privacy."[1] In this chapter I discuss the moral and legal challenges to privacy that arise in the context of two types of cases: (i) database information storage and (ii) new telephone and computer services such as caller identification and e-mail. These cases illustrate the importance of beginning with a presumption favoring privacy protection when such privacy interests are at stake, as well as showing how this strategy can be implemented effectively. I thus defend ways in which these new technologies can be managed so that consumers can reap the technological benefits and avoid forfeiting their privacy without their knowledge and consent.

Privacy and Electronic Databases

Consider first a case involving credit bureaus and the U.S. Post Office.[2] We now pay $.32 in the United States for a first-class postage stamp, more than double its price in 1960, even when adjusted for inflation. But those who are frustrated about paying more money for stamps may be even more concerned that raising rates is not the only step the U.S. Postal Service has considered taking to increase profits. The postal service has also studied plans to sell addresses, as part of the first nationwide electronic address list, to direct mail companies and other businesses. Unfortunately, this profit-seeking move is potentially very costly to consumers, as it risks major losses of individual privacy. The problem does not lie solely with the proposed address list. It is what businesses, investigators, and government can do by matching such a list with names and other information already for sale. The postal executives have claimed that the list will reduce undeliverable mail and that they will strictly control use of the list. We may well wonder why, then, the direct mail industry has become so excited at the prospect.

In America, when you request a store catalogue or file a change of address card or fill a prescription, your name goes on a list. When you apply for a mortgage, a driver's license, or telephone service, you part with private details about yourself and often supply extensive amounts of information. Virtually every transaction today is recorded in a computer, and a recent consequence is the routine collection and transfer of personal information in digitized form. The sale of such data for profit in the American private sector is now a multimillion-dollar business dominated by three leading credit bureaus: TRW in California, Equifax in Atlanta, and Trans Union Credit Information in Chicago. The sheer volume of information stored and repeatedly resold is stunning: these information sponges keep more than 400 million records on 160 million individuals. In 1988 TRW revenues were $335 million, with 155 million individual files; Trans Union revenues were $300 million with 155 million files; Equifax revenues were $269 million, with 100 million files—and they are not the only ones in the business.[3]

At little or no cost, the bureaus make it easy for almost anyone to find out another individual's income, employment status, marital status, driving record, real estate holdings, credit limit, and even civil and criminal court records. Yet it is difficult or impossible for individuals to find out if information about them is being used. A 1989 *Business Week* article described how

the long arm of American Express Co. reached out and grabbed Ray Parrish. After getting his credit card in January, the 22-year-old New Yorker promptly paid bills of $331 and $204.39 in February and March. Then he got a surprising call. His credit privileges were being suspended, an American Express clerk informed him, because his checking account showed too small a balance to pay his April charge of $596. A contrite American Express now says it should have asked before peeking, and it reinstated Parrish after he paid his bill from his savings and cash on hand. But that was beside the point. "I felt violated," says Parrish, who has kept his card because he needs it. "When I gave them my bank account number, I never thought they would use it to routinely look over my shoulder."[4]

TRW, Equifax, and Trans Union claim to guard their information, but they actually sell it readily. As a test, one of the editors of *Business Week*

signed up with two superbureaus, identifying himself as an editor at Mc-Graw-Hill Inc. He told one fib: that he might be hiring an employee or two and would need their credit reports. After a perfunctory check, both bureaus gave him carte blanche—and revealed the surprising breadth of their files. . . . Provided with just the names and addresses of two of his colleagues, one superbureau produced their credit reports—including their social security numbers that the editor didn't have—for $20 apiece. The superbureau manager warned that one colleague's mortgage was ominously large, then offered to fax the reports.

The second arrangement was more open-ended. For a $500 initial fee, the editor got access via his home computer to the superbureau's data base. Free to explore, he again checked on his colleagues, at about $15 per report. Then, he ran two names whose prominence might have set off alarms if the credit agency audited the use of its files. One was Representative Richard J. Durbin (D-Ill.), the other Dan Quayle [who was vice president at the time].

There were no alarms. . . . There was nothing juicy.[5]

The editor learned that Quayle charges more at Sears, Roebuck than at Brooks Brothers and has a big mortgage; he was also given all Quayle's credit card numbers. When told of the search, Quayle was not amused.

There are at least four sets of privacy problems generated by these huge credit bureau databases. First, once one is in a database in the United States, one loses access to and control over the information. There are few legal restrictions at present, and a great deal of money can be made by selling data. Economic and market factors make the information vulnerable to exposure. What one may have thought was private, such as shopping and spending habits or medical problems, soon can become public. Consider, for example, the dangers that can accompany advances in genetic testing. Tests for breast cancer genes, to cite one case, could potentially be extremely useful for patients who might benefit from extra vigilance to check for the disease. If confidentiality of the results cannot be assured, however, allowing the information to be part of a doctor's or genetic counselor's file could mean that patients are later identified as having "preexisting conditions," jeopardizing medical insurance coverage for themselves and even their children.

Second, there are many loopholes in current legal protections. That is, there is a serious *lack* of protection despite statutory attempts to salvage privacy. As a writer at *Business Week* observes,

The Fair Credit Reporting Act of 1970 is a case in point. It sounds good. It gives individuals the right to see and correct their credit reports and limits the rights of others to look at them. But it has five exceptions, including a big one: Anyone with a "legitimate business need" can peek. Legitimate isn't defined.

Then there's the Right to Financial Privacy Act of 1978. It forbids the government to rummage through bank-account records without following set procedures. But it excludes state agencies, including law enforcement officials, as well as private employers. And more exceptions are tacked on every year.[6]

These loopholes minimize the effectiveness of the legislation. Moreover, the patchwork of legal protections is peculiar and difficult to justify. Rental records from a video store are protected, for example, while medical insurance records, which often contain more important and more personal information, are not. This is especially disturbing since Blue Cross/Blue Shield and other health care providers now require detailed explanations of treatment before granting even partial reimbursement, thus creating new medical data files for each payment.

Third, private individuals can now use personal computers and Internet services to gain access to database information. New software developed by TRW, Lotus Development Corporation, and others magnifies access to this information because of its low cost, ease of use, and lack of safeguards. What is more, these computer programs allow unlimited use of the information purchased. In addition, similar information is now available on-line, through privately held CDB Infotek in Santa Ana, California, and Information America in Atlanta. Both can be called on "800" numbers (voice lines), and searches conducted through these companies can yield information such as divorce records; mortgage, IRS, and other financial data; and even individual social security numbers.[7] It is unnerving to learn that a public agency such as the U.S. Postal Service would contemplate profiting from such efforts, by providing a single national address directory with no "unlisted" option. One can, of course, ask that one's name be removed from mailing lists. One can decline to provide information on certain forms. But there is no guarantee that one's name *will* be removed. Moreover, being added to a database is unavoidable when one applies for credit cards, gets a telephone, or enters a hospital, and one cannot dictate where and to whom the information goes.

To be fair, it is important to note that Lotus and Equifax have

withdrawn some of their prospective programs from the market—
namely, "Lotus Marketplace: Households" and "Lotus Marketplace: Businesses," which anyone could tap into with a personal
computer. These programs gave personal information on names
broken down by categories that included gender, age, marital
status, dwelling unit type, and shopping habits, on about 120 million households. After a storm of protest from 30,000 consumers,
the products were recalled.[8] Equifax has also said it is giving up
its controversial practice of selling target lists drawn from confidential credit files to purveyors of junk mail. These are clearly
major concessions to the growing public sentiment that electronic
databases and on-line services providing access to sensitive information are used in ways that threaten personal privacy. Yet other
data bureaus and Internet data services insist they have no plans
to reduce access to their information banks. And the store of data
continues to increase. Information from the U.S. census taken in
1990 was considerably more detailed than in the past. The most
recent census data on house values, family membership, ethnicity,
elderly needs, transportation habits, and educational level are
now available on CD-ROM and floppy disk, providing information
easily and inexpensively to direct marketers and others who can
access and convert the data into more usable formats.

Fourth, data once recorded rarely disappears. Yet obsolete information can be misleading or incriminating out of context.
Moreover, in any database, the information may be erroneous.
Surveys in 1988 and 1991 found errors in 43 to 48 percent of
credit reports, including as many as 19 percent with inaccuracies
that could lead to denial of credit.[9] Errors may not be the fault
of the credit bureaus. Sometimes an original public record is itself
inaccurate. Regardless of an error's source, however, there are no
clear or established procedures for correcting it. Simply finding
out if the information given out about oneself is inaccurate may
not be difficult. In 1996, TRW provided one free copy per year
of any individual's own credit file on request, and Equifax and
Trans Union charged a fee of only $8.00 for each report.[10] De-
spite easy access to files, however, many people have horror stories
about what happens after they discover an error. Correcting an

error may be nearly impossible. One man reportedly contacted a credit bureau repeatedly to correct erroneous information. Soon after, he was denied credit for a loan on the grounds that computer records of his frequent inquiries concerning his credit rating indicated he may well have been "tampering" with the information, and thus his high credit rating was viewed as unreliable!

Nevertheless, I believe steps can be taken to preserve privacy in the face of massive databases and on-line dispersal of information. The move by Lotus and Equifax to recall software allowing access to files via personal computer is encouraging. Apparently concerned with its image, Equifax has also hired Professor Alan Westin, a privacy expert from Columbia University, to review its privacy protections. Thus it is clear that public pressure can have an effect and *must* be continued.

In addition, we need better legislative controls over access to information. The European Union has proposed privacy guidelines to restrict carefully the collection and dissemination of personal data. These guidelines require companies to register all databases containing personal information, require that subjects be told and give consent for their personal data to be collected or used, and require that any information gained for one purpose not be used for any other purpose unless the individual consents after being given an opportunity to refuse to allow the information sharing. The guidelines also prevent transfer of information from one country to another unless the latter country also has adequate protection of records, and they do not allow collection of data on race, ethnic origin, political or religious affiliation, health status, or sexual orientation.[11] Europeans are astounded there is no comparable protection or similar plan pending in the United States. Unfortunately American corporations, far from embracing these sound ideas, are fearful that the rules will hinder their routine use of computer data. However, many European countries are threatening to prohibit business transactions with American companies that cannot ensure similar protection. Consequently, the profit motive may actually boost privacy protection in this area.

We should note that this American fear of regulating data may be unwarranted. Some argue that Germany's experience with careful control of electronic databases undermines U.S. marketers' claims that strict privacy laws will place unacceptable burdens on businesses. Today Germany is cited as having Europe's most successful direct marketing industry, despite laws that forbid collecting personal information on anyone without prior notification and withholding that information if the individual wants to review it. The German system requires businesses of twenty or more employees to name an official to oversee gathering of personal data. There are state and federal data directors as well.[12]

Sweden, which in 1973 was the first country to pass a national privacy law, provides a somewhat different example. It has a centralized government file with the information that marketers want, and the file is used by about 90 percent of Sweden's direct mail companies.[13] The worry with this centralization is that it places too much power in a single public agency. Advocates of the system reply that the constitutional right for any individual to see what is in the archives or files places a check on the government. Having access to information does not guarantee *control* over the information, however, and it is not clear what procedures Sweden has for those who find erroneous information or want data eliminated from their file.

Another proposal worth considering is the formation of national privacy boards staffed with experts who have considered the issues from consumer, business, political, philosophical, and economic viewpoints. These boards could oversee regulations such as those suggested by the European Union. They might also implement and supervise additional protective measures, such as provision of free annual credit reports to consumers and regular mandatory updates, audits, and corrections in reports.

Note, however, the common theme in these different approaches by the European Union, Germany, Sweden, and others. Each echoes a dominant thesis of this book: the initial *presumption* must be that privacy protection is important and guidelines are essential. Moreover, each plan helps individuals retain control over information about themselves by providing knowledge about the data banks and access to the information, and by requiring permission and consent for collection or transfer of data.

Dynamic Negotiation of Privacy for Caller ID and E-mail

The proliferation of privacy-invading technologies has outpaced legislation aimed at protecting our privacy rights. People want information about others but are reluctant to divulge it about themselves. Perhaps this conflict is most apparent in the telephone feature known as caller identification, or caller ID, which allows those receiving calls to see the telephone number and name of the caller before answering the phone. With this service offered by the seven Baby Bells, unsuspecting consumers can have their privacy invaded each time they pick up the phone.[14]

For several years, the telephone companies have been offering a service to direct mailers with "800" or "900" telephone numbers that routinely provides marketers with end-of-the-month lists of the phone numbers of all their callers, with no restrictions on the use of the information. Marketers often sell those lists to others seeking to target new customers. The service is rapidly expanding: thanks to technology now being developed, all callers can be identified by their phone numbers to whomever they call, even if their numbers are unlisted in a telephone directory. It is simple: for as little as $6.50 a month as a service fee, plus a one-time equipment charge of $29 to $80, customers can install on their phone an electronic screen that flashes *every* incoming number while the phone is still ringing. Telephone companies can also deliver the name, as well as the number, of the incoming caller, and that is quickly becoming the service norm. Caller ID was first introduced in the United States by Bell Atlantic in New Jersey in 1987. By the end of 1991 it was approved in over twenty states and under consideration in thirteen others.[15]

Some legal theorists have argued that the privacy interests at stake in the use of caller ID are moderate, claiming that the technology does not raise significant privacy concerns.[16] Justice Stewart's comments in his dissent in *Smith v. Maryland* express the contrary opinion:

It simply is not enough to say, after *Katz*, that there is no legitimate expectation of privacy in the numbers dialed because the caller assumes the risk that the telephone company will disclose them. . . . Most private telephone subscribers may have their own numbers listed in a publicly distributed directory, but I doubt that there are any who would be happy to have broadcast to the world a list of the local or long distance numbers they have called. This is not because such a list might in some sense be incriminating, but because it easily could reveal the identities of the persons and the places called, and thus reveal the most intimate details of a person's life.[17]

Justice Stewart's view has been endorsed and expanded by the American Civil Liberties Union[18] and by the 1986 Electronic Communications Privacy Act (ECPA). In the ECPA, Congress rejected the *Smith v. Maryland* conclusion that telephone toll records are not entitled to privacy protection. Furthermore, the Congressional Research Service has interpreted the ECPA prohibitions to apply to caller ID subscribers.[19] Clearly, the privacy issues surrounding caller ID systems are serious and need to be addressed more fully.

Whenever you call someone with caller ID, your privacy is at risk. Whether you know it or not, anyone with the service has easy and immediate access to your phone number and often your name. Even worse, sophisticated new software matches your number to various databases, allowing your files to be displayed on a computer screen as fast as your call can be connected. A major danger is the appropriation and misuse of your credit history or your employment or medical records by anyone with caller ID and a computer—an insurance company, banking or lending firm, or potential employer. In a world of endless computer links, massive data banks, and Internet information highways, increasingly vast amounts of personal information are compiled and accessed without our knowledge or consent. Privacy issues surrounding caller ID are magnified because the telephone companies offering the service are, in an almost Orwellian fashion, becoming increasingly powerful keepers and purveyors of information most of us consider private. Recent court decisions have cleared the way for the Baby Bells to enter the electronic information services business, using phone lines to provide news reports and stock quotes, as well as long-term storage of business and medical records.[20] Now they have the power to package and publish electronic information for sale across business and home phone lines in ways we cannot control, to everyone from prospective employers to telemarketers, making the phone companies ever more powerful as the scope of telecommunications grows.

Protecting individual privacy without losing the benefits of caller ID is a difficult challenge. The telephone companies, in a stroke of marketing genius, have portrayed caller ID as a public service, and they are installing caller ID throughout the country. But as currently offered, caller ID generates phone company profits while infringing privacy on both ends of the line and pitting privacy advocates who support call recipients against privacy advocates who support callers. On one hand, proponents of the technology argue that it provides a valuable service to people pestered by obscene or harassing phone calls or persistent telemarketers, as well as to delivery services such as florists who need verification for orders or who are plagued by pranksters. The benefits are obvious: caller ID lets them know who is calling before they answer the phone. On the other hand, privacy advocates for callers vehemently disagree, maintaining that callers have privacy rights, too, and should be able to choose anonymity. They worry that the prospect of identification will deter anonymous police informants or callers to hotlines for drug abusers, people with AIDS, or runaways, for instance. They believe caller ID can threaten the safety of those trying to find refuge from batterers or child abusers and will discourage doctors and other professionals from returning emergency calls from their homes, fearing release of their private numbers.

Opponents of caller ID believe few of us want our names and numbers automatically available for direct callbacks, and they know information about who calls a number can easily be used to compile and update telemarketing lists and data banks. They recognize that the cost of caller ID puts it beyond the reach of low-income customers, further aggravating inequalities of power.

As Pennsylvania ACLU Executive Director Barry Steinhardt has argued, "Not only does the use of Caller ID go against public policy, but it is one more blatant example of how emerging technology is stripping away individual privacy rights layer by layer."[21] Generally, when people see themselves as receivers of phone calls, they are eager for caller ID. But as callers, most want the power to block display of their numbers and names. Ironically, the privacy interests compete within the same people: those who both make and receive telephone calls.

The privacy problems of caller ID are amplified in part by a similar telephone service called ANI (automatic number identification) geared to businesses, including those with toll-free numbers. Like caller ID, ANI passes a telephone number along with each call, and then matches the number with a customer's corporate database in a personal computer, making it possible for a caller's file to be displayed before anyone answers the phone.[22] Beginning with just a phone number, a whole host of information becomes common property.

Unfortunately, most parties to the debate over caller ID have taken extreme positions. They either recommend that the service be legally prohibited, revoked, or heavily regulated to protect privacy, or they defend caller ID as a service that should be available with no limitations. There is, however, a logical and intuitive way to use this technology in a way that can satisfy both camps in the privacy debate. This new way of thinking about privacy regulation, described by Ross Mitchell as "dynamic negotiation," permits the enjoyment of the benefits of new telecommunications technologies—including but not limited to caller ID—without sacrificing individual privacy.[23]

Most caller ID systems automatically release the caller's phone number and name. To prevent this information from being divulged for a particular call, the caller must enter a code (typically *67) before dialing the number. In other words, callers must take an extra step each time they want to retain the privacy that they had previously taken for granted. This is known as "per-call" blocking. Even in U.S. Representative Edward J. Markey's proposed "privacy bill of rights," callers can only block the transmission of their number on a per-call basis. Some phone systems allow "per-line" blocking: the caller's number is kept private by default and is released only when the caller enters an "unblocking" code for a single call. A serious difficulty is that for most caller ID systems, automatic supply of phone numbers is routine. Blocking, if available at all, is usually allowed only on a per-call basis. With these systems the burden for blocking is always on the caller. Callers must know that their numbers are being released, must learn how to block the release, and must remember to enter the special code every time they want to block automatic transmission of their phone numbers. Hence callers cannot avoid "assuming the risk" of privacy loss without careful self-discipline. Bell Atlantic, among other providers, has been fighting *all* blocking on the grounds that it will devalue their service.[24] In 1992, New England Telephone chose not to offer caller ID rather than be forced to provide a blocking option. Under pressure from the Massachusetts Department of Public Utilities, New England Telephone reversed its policy but at first offered per-call blocking as the only option. For other telephone companies as well, per-line blocking is either unavailable or must be specially requested by the customer.[25]

In a preposterous example of the profit motive at work, New York Telephone, in a full-page letter in the *New York Times*, defended caller ID with blocking on a single-call basis as a public service valuable for consumers, society, and the telephone companies.[26] It insisted that caller ID can help deter crimes such as bomb threats and kidnapping, arguing that per-call blocking by code adequately protects the privacy of callers as well as those subscribing to the service. New York Telephone maintained, furthermore, that per-line blocking increases false alarms and compromises the effectiveness of emergency response agencies such as police, fire, and ambulance services by impeding quick determination of call sources. It claimed that children and others would either forget or not know how to disengage the blocking in an emergency. This appeal to public policy is both self-serving and deceptive. The phone companies are well aware that the technology is available to override blocking for "911" calls and other emergency numbers. Moreover, with the responsibility on the caller to safeguard privacy on every call, privacy is lost by default. Note also that there is a widely available telephone service called Call Trace; though less well known and less well advertised it is more effective than caller ID for combating obscene and harassing phone calls. As attorney Janlori Goldman explains, "With Call Trace, a person who receives such a call can instantly send a signal to the phone company and the police that records the phone number of the caller and alerts law enforcement officials that the call was just received. Most importantly, *Call Trace is still effective even if the caller blocks.*"[27]

The Pennsylvania Supreme Court barred caller ID in 1990, ruling that it violates the state's wiretap laws and the state's constitutional right to privacy. Reversing an order from the Pennsylvania Public Utilities Commission, the court argued that "Caller ID, either in its blockable or unblockable format, violates the privacy rights of the people of this commonwealth."[28] By 1995, Massachusetts and New York regulators insisted that Nynex offer customers a choice of per-call or per-line blocking. Nevertheless, most proposed federal legislation on caller ID at that time supported the phone companies by failing to mandate the option of per-line blocking, thus leaving the burden of blocking on the consumer.

The Federal Communications Commission has argued that the potential public value of caller ID outweighs the privacy concerns of those who want automatic blocking of numbers and it has called per-line blocking "unduly burdensome." In 1995 the commission proposed regulations requiring that on interstate calls, only per-call blocking would be permitted, preempting state regulations that allowed per-line blocking. In a concession, FCC regulations in effect by 1996 required per-call blocking and allowed per-line blocking where state policies permit it. But consumers must know about and understand the options in order to select per-line blocking, and they must live in a state that allows it. Experts say that so far, few people are blocking release of their numbers. That is no surprise. Even careful readers can overlook or misunderstand inserts in phone bills that describe blocking, and consequently much of the public is unaware of the option to block.

It seems clear that caller ID, like computer databases, must be regulated at the federal rather than local level, perhaps with worldwide guidelines to follow. This is necessary in part to coordinate the interstate calling patterns of consumers and businesses, as well as to harmonize the competing claims of individual privacy and commercial viability. Local or state regulations do not protect privacy uniformly, and they will undoubtedly lead consumers to become frustrated or annoyed with a patchwork of different rules and options. Such frustration will only hinder the success of the technology. There is, moreover, a better alternative for satisfying both parties in the privacy debate over caller ID: namely, to provide per-line blocking as the standard service, with a choice to revert to per-call blocking. This can be accomplished in a way that allows people dynamically to negotiate the degree of privacy they wish to sacrifice or maintain.

Consider how such a system would work with caller ID. Initially, all phone subscribers' lines would, by default, block the release of the caller's number. Subscribers could choose to release their number on a per-call basis by dialing an unblocking code (other than *67). Thus far, this is just per-line blocking. But phones with caller ID displays could also be set up automatically to refuse calls when the number has not been provided by the caller. When an anonymous call is attempted, the phone does not ring. The thwarted caller hears a short recorded message explaining that to complete the call, the originating phone number must be furnished. This message then instructs the caller what code to dial to give out the number. Otherwise, the call is incomplete and the caller is not charged. Thus, a caller has the chance to decide whether a call is important enough that it is worth surrendering anonymity. This solution preserves choice and ensures privacy. Callers can control when to give out their numbers; call recipients can screen and refuse anonymous calls. The system remains voluntary. Through a dynamic and interactive process, both callers and call recipients are allowed to determine the extent to which their privacy is compromised.

Most callers, of course, will want to release their number when calling friends and associates. And if such calls dominate their use of the phone, they might choose to change the default on their line so that it automatically releases their number unless they dial in a blocking code. Thus, a dynamic negotiation system may well lead many people to change from per-line to per-call blocking—precisely what the phone companies and the FCC favor. But when these customers change their default setting, they will know what they are choosing and why; they will be actively consenting to give out their numbers as a matter of course. Most businesses will want to take all calls, whether numbers are provided or not. But certain establishments might want to reject anonymous calls—for example, pizzerias that want incoming numbers for verification to avoid filling bogus orders. Most callers will happily unblock their numbers when such a business asks them to do so.

Some display units that can be purchased for use with caller ID are already able to reject anonymous calls, but they are a far cry from the dynamic negotiation system described. With these caller ID units, every call, whether accepted or not, is considered to have been answered and is charged to the caller. But a call that is rejected because of its anonymity should entail no charge. This requires that the call be intercepted by the phone company's central office switchboard before it reaches the recipient's line. The technology for implementing dynamic negotiation for caller ID is already available. The FCC need only amend its recent ruling and mandate per-line blocking as the default. If the FCC refuses, the House Telecommunications Subcommittee should propose legislation to require dynamic negotiation. With this system as the national norm, privacy concerns associated with caller ID would become self-regulating.

Although inspired by the debate over caller ID, the concept of dynamic negotiation of privacy can apply to other telecommunications technologies. One likely target is electronic mail. With traditional paper mail, people have always had the right, and the ability, to send anonymous correspondence. Delivery of the envelope requires neither that the letter be signed nor that a return address be provided. On the receiving end, people similarly have the right to discard anonymous mail unopened. Applying the principles of dynamic negotiation, senders of electronic mail would have the option to identify or not identify themselves. Recipients could reject as undeliverable any e-mail with an unidentified sender. The sender would then have the option to retransmit the message, this time with a return address. As with caller ID, the users negotiate among themselves. The system itself remains privacy neutral.

The fundamental presumption is that privacy must be viewed as important from multiple perspectives; its protection should be assumed to be necessary at the outset, and technology should be so adapted that its use does not automatically require that one forfeit one's privacy. Several criteria guide the approach I have defended: (i) the need to protect individual privacy for all parties to a communication, (ii) the importance of letting new technologies flourish, and (iii) the need for national guidelines to provide consistency in system use and privacy protection where we now have a conglomeration of conflicting state guidelines. Since technological innovation proceeds rapidly, we must continually examine how best to make possible new features while preserving or enhancing our existing privacy. Congress and the FCC must shed their laissez-faire attitude and endorse privacy as essential to telecommunications technology. Consumers must demand that the government make it possible to easily protect the privacy of both the caller and the called, the e-mail sender and receiver. Individuals, not the telephone or communications companies, should determine the manner and extent to which the new information technologies pervade our nation.

This new concept of a dynamic implementation of information technology can be broadly applied. When technological advance clashes with privacy, it is imperative to seek a solution in which the technology does not dictate the extent of privacy protection, but instead the consumers and targeted individuals choose when and how much to protect or relinquish their privacy. For caller ID and e-mail, as well as in the European proposals for regulating databases, the key idea is to maintain the *presumption* in favor of privacy. That is, begin with maximal privacy protection and then ensure that people are educated, consulted, and allowed to give consent or refusal before information is gathered or disseminated. They may then choose whether or not it is worthwhile for

them to release personal database information or their phone
numbers, addresses, and so on. The challenge is to find a balance
that will protect privacy comprehensively, but not at the expense
of technological services.

I have focused in this chapter on only two instances where
information technology and privacy collide. Many other cases
arise where there is a need to balance access to information and
privacy. For example: Should doctors know when patients have
AIDS or are HIV positive? Should patients be told the HIV status
of doctors?[29] Who, for what reasons, should be allowed access to
the results of genetic testing? How much employment monitoring, through closed-circuit television, phone tapping, e-mail and
computer files, is acceptable? Are tracking and surveillance systems for criminal suspects justified? Surely there are many others.

There are a number of moral issues that arise from conflicts
between privacy and information technology. First, technological
advances without restrictions often erase one's ability to maintain
privacy and control information about oneself. Second, competing claims between public access and individual privacy are sometimes compounded by concerns over the coercive power of the
state. We want to live in an open and accountable society, yet we
also want to preserve our right to be let alone. Third, one person's
or one group's right to know often collides with another's right
to keep information private. It is difficult to make broad generalizations about how to balance these interests. Individuals may
make different choices based on their evaluation of the context
of each case, and it is essential to involve them in the decisions
wherever possible.

Legal issues are rapidly emerging in this area as well. In some
cases, there are as yet no legal guidelines to help answer questions
about how much is private, as with doctors who are HIV positive
and want to withhold that information. In other cases, there is a
patchwork of local regulations that conflict, as in different U.S.
state laws concerning the telephone companies and caller ID. Finally, there are cases where national regulations and legislation
have been proposed and passed, but where there are loopholes

or escape clauses that vitiate the intended effects of the legislation, as is the case with U.S. statutes on databases and information storage.

There are many good reasons to keep public records open and accessible. It is important for society to monitor illegal activities, to capture criminals, and to preserve public safety. Oliver North's e-mail messages helped lead to major revelations in the Iran-Contra scandal, and organized crime leaders have been detected through phone taps and surveillance. Yet personal data can be collected and used to blackmail people, as was done by J. Edgar Hoover and the FBI in the 1960s and 1970s, ruining innocent lives.[30] Clearly individual privacy must be balanced against other rights and values, such as public safety. It is sometimes difficult to separate trivial irritations arising from privacy intrusions, such as extra junk mail, from more damaging privacy invasions. But it is also worth remembering that technology and privacy need not be incompatible and antagonistic. Airport X-ray machines can make hand searches of luggage less frequent. Magnetic markers in books and on merchandise make searches of briefcases and bags in libraries and stores largely unnecessary. Our goal should be to manage new technologies appropriately, not impede or destroy them.

The approach I have defended throughout this book requires first that we specify which types of matters are private, as outlined in chapter 4. Surely aspects of one's medical history may legitimately be viewed as private, in contrast to information one voluntarily provides to a newspaper. Second, we must maintain a presumption in favor of privacy and then develop criteria for deciding whether a violation of privacy is justified. As discussed in the chapter 8, random drug testing for airline pilots may be a clear invasion of privacy, but it may be justified on the basis of public safety if there is strong evidence of drug abuse related to accidents and reasonable likelihood the testing can help alleviate the problem. In contrast, random testing of clerical workers is not legitimate when their work can be monitored in other ways without violating their privacy. In the case of address lists and phone numbers, local firehouses or ambulance services may need this information to respond immediately to emergencies and save lives. And financial institutions clearly have legitimate uses for credit histories in an era of economic stress and increased bankruptcies. But free-flowing information on interconnected public or private databases that can be sold without restrictions is not only highly questionable but extremely intrusive.

I have argued in this book that privacy has played a meaningful conceptual role in political, religious, biological, anthropological, and sociological contexts and that narrow conceptions or definitions of privacy in law and philosophy neither match nor explain important intuitions about our privacy interests. Privacy, broadly characterized as a complex of three related clusters of claims concerning information, access, and activities, is valuable because it shields us from interference and threats of intrusion, scrutiny, ridicule, pressure to conform, and the losses they may bring, whether these are due to access to information, access to one's physical person, or an attempt to restrict one's behavior. While care must be taken to avoid allowing privacy as a cover for abuse, privacy is nevertheless essential for protecting the freedom and independence needed for individuals to develop their identities and values as self-conscious beings. After defending this broad conception of privacy against the feminist critique of privacy as well as arguments critical of constitutional privacy, I have discussed privacy cases with implications for reproductive choice and the legislation of morals. These last two chapters demonstrate that it is indeed possible to protect privacy stringently in the face of advancing technologies and pressures to protect public safety. More self-regulation, systems of dynamic negotiation, and new legislative guidelines *can* prevent what often appears to be an inevitable erosion of privacy.

Notes

Introduction

1 In a controversial decision the California Supreme Court answered negatively. *Tarasoff v. Regents of University of California*, 17 Cal. 3d 425 (1976).

2 Hyman Gross, "The Concept of Privacy," 42 *New York University Law Review* 34 (1967).

3 William Parent, "A New Definition of Privacy for the Law," *Law and Philosophy* 2 (1983), 305–338; Parent, "Privacy, Morality, and the Law," *Philosophy and Public Affairs* 12 (1983), 269–288; Louis Henkin, "Privacy and Autonomy," 74 *Columbia Law Review* 1410 (1974).

4 Richard Posner, "Uncertain Protection of Privacy by the Supreme Court," 1979 *Supreme Court Review* 173, 214 (1979).

5 Judith Jarvis Thomson, "The Right to Privacy," *Philosophy and Public Affairs* 4 (1975), 295–314, reprinted in Ferdinand David Schoeman, ed., *Philosophical Dimensions of Privacy: An Anthology* (Cambridge: Cambridge University Press, 1984), 272–289.

6 Thomas Scanlon, "Thomson on Privacy," *Philosophy and Public Affairs* 4 (1975), 315–322; Jeffrey Reiman, "Privacy, Intimacy, and Personhood," *Philosophy and Public Affairs* 6 (1976), 26–44, reprinted in Schoeman, ed., *Philosophical Dimensions of Privacy*, 300–316.

7 Julie Inness, *Privacy, Intimacy, and Isolation* (Oxford: Oxford University Press, 1992). See also Robert S. Gerstein, "Intimacy and Privacy," *Ethics* 89 (1978), 76–81, reprinted in Schoeman, ed., *Philosophical Dimensions of Privacy*, 265–271.

8 *Whalen v. Roe*, 429 U.S. 589, 599, 600 (1977).

9 Catharine MacKinnon, *Toward a Feminist Theory of the State* (Cambridge: Harvard University Press, 1989).

10 John Hart Ely, "The Wages of Crying Wolf: A Comment on *Roe v. Wade*," 82 *Yale Law Journal* 920 (1973).

11 John Hart Ely, *Democracy and Distrust: A Theory of Judicial Review* (Cambridge: Harvard University Press, 1980).

12 *Bowers v. Hardwick*, 478 U.S. 186 (1986).

13 Patrick Devlin, *The Enforcement of Morals* (Oxford: Oxford University Press, 1965), and H. L. A. Hart, "Immorality and Treason," *The Listener*, July 1959, 162–163.

1. Origins and History of Privacy

[1] I am indebted to Sissela Bok for stressing the importance of this point and for providing helpful sources for this discussion.

[2] Jean Bethke Elshtain, *Public Man, Private Woman: Women in Social and Political Thought* (Princeton: Princeton University Press, 1981), 9.

[3] Aristotle, *The Politics*, translated by Benjamin Jowett, in *The Basic Works of Aristotle*, ed. Richard McKeon (New York: Random House, 1941), 1127–1324.

[4] Jürgen Habermas, *The Structural Transformation of the Public Sphere*, trans. Thomas Burger and Frederick Lawrence (Cambridge: MIT Press, 1962), reprinted in part in Richard C. Turkington, George B. Trubow, and Anita L. Allen, eds., *Privacy: Cases and Materials* (Houston, Tex: John Marshall, 1992), 3.

[5] Aristotle, *The Politics*, esp. 1129–1136.

[6] John Locke, *The Second Treatise on Government*, ed. Thomas P. Peardon, (New York: Macmillan, Library of Liberal Arts, 1988), 4.

[7] See Elshtain, *Public Man, Private Woman*, 121, for a discussion of the implications of this reading of the relationship between public and private realms for the roles of men and women in Locke's civil society. For another discussion of the public and private in Locke's works, see Carole Pateman, *The Disorder of Women: Democracy, Feminism, and Political Theory* (Stanford: Stanford University Press, 1989).

[8] Milton R. Konvitz, "Privacy and the Law: A Philosophical Prelude," *Law and Contemporary Problems* 31 (1966), 272.

[9] Alan Westin, "The Origins of Modern Claims to Privacy," in Ferdinand David Schoeman, ed., *Philosophical Dimensions of Privacy: An Anthology* (Cambridge: Cambridge University Press, 1984), 56–74.

[10] Ibid., 57. See also Peter H. Klopfer and Daniel I. Rubenstein, "The Concept *Privacy* and Its Biological Basis," *Journal of Social Issues: Privacy as a Behavioral Phenomenon* 33, 3 (1977), 52–65.

[11] Elshtain, *Public Man, Private Woman*, 6.

[12] See *Journal of Social Issues: Privacy as a Behavioral Phenomenon*, 33, 3 (1977) for a wide range of essays establishing privacy as a universal. See also Margaret Mead, *Coming of Age in Samoa* (New York: New American Library, 1949).

[13] Westin, "Origins of Modern Claims to Privacy," 59ff.

[14] *Journal of Social Issues: Privacy as a Behavioral Phenomenon*, 33, 3 (1977). See also Stanley I. Benn and Gerald Gaus, eds., *The Private and Public in Social Policy* (London: Croon Helm; New York: St. Martin's Press, 1983).

[15] Thomas C. Cooley, *Law of Torts* (1st ed. 1880, 2d ed., 1888).

[16] *DeMay v. Roberts*, 46 Mich. 160, 165–166, 9 N.W. 146, 149 (1881).

[17] Samuel Warren and Louis Brandeis, "The Right to Privacy," 4 *Harvard*

Law Review 193 (1890), reprinted in Schoeman, ed., *Philosophical Dimensions of Privacy*, 75–103.

[18] *Winsmore v. Greenbank*, Willes 577 (1745).

[19] Warren and Brandeis, "The Right to Privacy," 215.

[20] Ibid., 195.

[21] William L. Prosser, "Privacy," 48 *California Law Review* 383 (1960).

[22] Warren and Brandeis, "The Right to Privacy," 213 n.

[23] Ibid., 201, 205.

[24] *Roberson v. Rochester Folding Box Company*, 171 N.Y. 538 (1902). The defendant had admittedly used lithographs of plaintiff's portrait without her consent to advertise its flour. But the New York Court of Appeals refused to recognize legal protection of privacy as part of common law in New York.

[25] In *Pavesich v. New England Life Insurance Company*, 122 Ga. 190 (1905), the Georgia Supreme Court declared the right of privacy to be part of Georgia law.

[26] Prosser, "Privacy," 389. Prosser's suggested third tort protection against publicity placing one in a false light is rarely invoked because of its overlap with defamation.

[27] Edward J. Bloustein, "Privacy as an Aspect of Human Dignity: An Answer to Dean Prosser," 39 *New York University Law Review* 962 (1964), reprinted in Schoeman, ed., *Philosophical Dimensions of Privacy*, 156–202.

[28] *Ex parte Jackson*, 96 U.S. 727 (1877).

[29] *Boyd v. United States*, 116 U.S. 616 (1886).

[30] *Olmstead v. United States*, 277 U.S. 438 (1928).

[31] Idem at 478.

[32] Bloustein, "An Answer to Dean Prosser," 976–977.

[33] *Berger v. New York*, 388 U.S. 41 (1967).

[34] *Katz v. United States*, 389 U.S. 347 (1967).

[35] Alan Westin, "Science, Privacy, and Freedom," 66 *Columbia Law Review* 1003 (1966).

[36] *United States v. White*, 401 U.S. 745 (1971); *United States v. Miller*, 425 U.S. 4335 (1976); *Smith v. Maryland*, 442 U.S. 735 (1979).

[37] See state court cases such as *People v. Beavers*, 393 Mich. 554 (1974) for an expansive approach that there is a search whenever privacy is encroached upon in a direct and substantial way.

[38] Turkington, Trubow, and Allen, *Privacy*, 104. These are of course just two examples of values balanced against privacy.

[39] Richard A. Posner, "An Economic Theory of Privacy," *Regulation*, May–June 1978 at 19, 25.

[40] *Griswold v. Connecticut*, 381 U.S. 479 (1965). The Court stated that the physicians were being prosecuted as accessories to the crime of contracep-

tive use and therefore had the legal standing to challenge, on behalf of married couples, the features of the law that made such use a crime.

41 For a discussion of this connection, see Turkington, Trubow, and Allen, *Privacy*, 231.

42 Ibid., 232.

43 Justice Goldberg defended the Ninth Amendment argument, a tough job since the amendment is often the brunt of legal jokes: viz., "when all else fails, cite the Ninth."

44 *Loving v. Virginia*, 388 U.S. 1 (1967).

45 *Stanley v. Georgia*, 394 U.S. 557 (1969).

46 *Eisenstadt v. Baird*, 405 U.S. 438, 453 (1972).

47 *Roe v. Wade*, 410 U.S. 113 (1973).

48 *Moore v. City of East Cleveland*, 431 U.S. 494 (1977).

49 *Pierce v. Society of Sisters*, 268 U.S. 510 (1925).

50 *Skinner v. Oklahoma*, 316 U.S. 535 (1942). Oklahoma's Habitual Criminal Sterilization Act provided for compulsory sterilization after a third conviction for a felony involving "moral turpitude" but excluded such felonies as embezzlement. Even if it had applied merely to sex offenders, it would still likely have been overturned based on the majority's argument that the legislation dealt with marriage and procreation, fundamental to the very existence and survival of the race. But note that *Buck v. Bell*, 274 U.S. 200 (1927), upheld the state of Virginia's power to perform sterilization against a woman's objection to prevent the birth of what Justice Holmes called "imbeciles." The law upheld continued to be implemented for almost fifty years. Over 7,500 involuntary sterilizations were performed by Virginia between 1924 and 1972, according to data cited in Stephen Jay Gould, *The Mismeasure of Man* (New York: Norton, 1981), 335.

51 *Akron v. Akron Center for Reproductive Health*, 426 U.S. 416 (1983).

52 *Harris v. McRae*, 488 U.S. 297 (1980).

53 *Planned Parenthood of Central Missouri v. Danforth*, 428 U.S. 52 (1976).

54 *Whalen v. Roe*, 429 U.S. 589 (1977).

55 *Bowers v. Hardwick*, 478 U.S. 186 (1986).

56 429 U.S. at 599, 600. The wording of clause (ii) helps show why there has been confusion over the relationship between privacy and autonomy.

57 With respect to the first privacy interest, the Court urged that the limited disclosure of information to state health workers was similar to other routine invasions of privacy associated with health care, suggesting that broad dissemination would be more problematic. Of the second interest, Justice Stevens argued that even with the statute in place, 100,000 prescriptions a month were filled for the drugs involved, demonstrating that the statute did not discourage independent decision making by deterring patients from seeking needed medications. This book will make clear that there are good reasons to question both arguments.

2. Narrow Views of Privacy Developed from the Law

1 William A. Parent, "A New Definition of Privacy for the Law," *Law and Philosophy* 2 (1983) 305–338; "Privacy, Morality, and the Law," *Philosophy and Public Affairs* 12 (1983), 269–288. See also Parent, "Recent Work on the Concept of Privacy," *American Philosophical Quarterly* 20 (1983), 341–356. Louis Henkin, "Privacy and Autonomy," 74 *Columbia Law Review* 1410 (1974). See also Hyman Gross, "Privacy and Autonomy," in J. Roland Pennock and John W. Chapman, eds. *Privacy*, Nomos 13 (New York: Atherton Press, 1971), 169–181. John Hart Ely, "The Wages of Crying Wolf: A Comment on *Roe v. Wade*," 82 *Yale Law Journal* 920 (1973).

2 *Griswold v. Connecticut*, 381 U.S. 479 (1965).

3 Joel Feinberg, *Social Philosophy* (Englewood Cliffs, N.J.: Prentice-Hall, 1973), 64–67.

4 Parent, "Privacy, Morality, and the Law," 269. See also Parent, "A New Definition of Privacy," 306. For another critique of Parent's view, see Jeffrey L. Johnson, "Privacy and the Judgment of Others," *Journal of Value Inquiry* 23 (1989), 157–168.

5 Parent, "Privacy, Morality, and the Law," 270; Parent, "A New Definition of Privacy," 307.

6 Judith Jarvis Thomson, "The Right to Privacy," *Philosophy and Public Affairs* 4 (1975), 295–314, esp. 308–313, reprinted in Ferdinand David Schoeman, ed., *Philosophical Dimensions of Privacy: An Anthology* (Cambridge: Cambridge University Press, 1984), 272–289. I borrow the term "reductionist" from Ruth Gavison, "Privacy and the Limits of Law," 89 *Yale Law Journal* 421 (1980), reprinted in Schoeman, ed., *Philosophical Dimensions of Privacy*, 346–402.

7 Others include Frederick Davis, "What Do We Mean by 'Right to Privacy'?" 4 *South Dakota Law Review* 1 (1959); Henry Kalven, Jr., "Privacy in Tort Law—Were Warren and Brandeis Wrong?" *Law and Contemporary Problems* 31 (1966), 326–341, who argues that tort protection from emotional harm, first defended by Warren and Brandeis (see n. 10), protects hypersensitivity; and Richard Posner, "The Right to Privacy," 12 *Georgia Law Review* 393 (1978), who suggests privacy claims indicate an unjustified wish to manipulate and defraud.

8 For similar criticisms of Thomson's account, see Thomas Scanlon, "Thomson on Privacy," *Philosophy and Public Affairs* 4 (1975), 315–322; Jeffrey Reiman, "Privacy, Intimacy, and Personhood," *Philosophy and Public Affairs* 6 (1976), 26–44, reprinted in Schoeman, ed., *Philosophical Dimensions of Privacy*, 300–316.

9 See Stanley I. Benn and Gerald Gaus, eds., *The Private and Public in Social Policy* (London: Croon Helm; New York: St. Martin's Press, 1983), and *Journal of Social Issues: Privacy as a Behavioral Phenomenon* 33, 3 (1977), especially Irwin Altman, "Privacy Regulation: Culturally Specific?" 66–84,

and Herbert Kelman, "Privacy and Research with Human Beings," 169–195, for descriptions of the variability of privacy protection in other societies.

10 "The right to one's person may be said to be a right of complete immunity: to be let alone" (Thomas C. Cooley, *Law of Torts*, 29 [2d ed., 1888]). Contrary to Parent's claim that Warren and Brandeis were the first to advocate this definition, they relied on Cooley's phrase as well as on cases they felt were already precedents to argue that the law should "protect the privacy of private life" by securing for an individual the right of determining the extent to which his written work, thoughts, sentiments, or likeness could be given to the public, a right they viewed as only part of the right to be let alone. See Samuel Warren and Louis Brandeis, "The Right to Privacy," 4 *Harvard Law Review* 193 (1890), esp. 215, reprinted in Schoeman, ed., *Philosophical Dimensions of Privacy*, 75–103.

11 Parent, "A New Definition of Privacy," 308.

12 *Briscoe v. Reader's Digest Association*, 4 Cal. 3d 529 (1971); *Melvin v. Reid*, 112 Cal. App. 283 (1931).

13 Parent, "Privacy, Morality, and the Law," 271.

14 Parent could defend his descriptive definition and discuss what ought or ought not be part of the public record, but he does not do so.

15 Parent, "Privacy, Morality, and the Law," 285.

16 Ibid., 280. It might be helpful to distinguish two sorts of unsuccessful spying. Suppose, for example, that B taps A's phone because B wants information about A's love life. B may fail in two ways: (i) the tap may not work at all; (ii) the tap works, but B fails to get the desired information. In the second case B has still acquired information about A, but not in the first.

17 Others who have characterized privacy almost exclusively in terms of the amount of information known about an individual include Charles Fried, *An Anatomy of Values* (Cambridge: Harvard University Press, 1970), 140; Arthur Miller, *The Assault on Privacy* (Cambridge: Harvard University Press, 1971), 25; Alan Westin, *Privacy and Freedom* (New York: Atheneum Press, 1967), 7; and Elizabeth Beardsley, "Privacy, Autonomy, and Selective Disclosure," in Pennock and Chapman, eds., *Privacy*, 56–70.

18 Paul Bender, "Privacy," in Norman Dorsen, ed., *Our Endangered Rights: The ACLU Report on Civil Liberties Today* (New York: Pantheon, 1984), 237–258.

19 Gavison, "Privacy and the Limits of the Law," 429–430.

20 I am indebted to Hilde Nelson for this example.

21 Scanlon, "Thomson on Privacy," 317. Scanlon has suggested that Parent might argue that this is a violation of a right to privacy even if it is not a case when privacy is diminished. Yet Parent denies privacy is relevant at all.

22 This is not to say that harassment and trespass, for example, never involve privacy intrusions as well, but they certainly do not always entail them.

[23] Hyman Gross, "The Concept of Privacy," 42 *New York University Law Review* 34, 35, 42 (1967).

[24] Richard Posner, "Uncertain Protection of Privacy by the Supreme Court," 1979 *Supreme Court Review* 173, 214 (1979).

[25] Ely, "The Wages of Crying Wolf," 931.

[26] Henkin, "Privacy and Autonomy," 1424–1425. As Henkin acknowledges, Hyman Gross makes a similar claim in his "Privacy and Autonomy," 180–181.

[27] On "negative liberty," see Isaiah Berlin, *Four Essays on Liberty* (Oxford: Oxford University Press, 1969).

[28] David A. J. Richards, *Toleration and the Constitution: A Theory of Religious Freedom, Free Speech, and Constitutional Privacy* (Oxford: Oxford University Press, 1986).

[29] Henkin, "Privacy and Autonomy," 1427. See Ely, "The Wages of Crying Wolf."

[30] For an explanation of the substantive due process doctrine, see the last section of this chapter.

[31] Thomas Huff, "Thinking Clearly about Privacy," 55 *Washington Law Review* 777, 785 (1980).

[32] *Whalen v. Roe*, 429 U.S. 589 (1977). See also June Aline Eichbaum, "Towards an Autonomy-Based Theory of Constitutional Privacy," 14 *Harvard Civil Rights–Civil Liberties Law Review* 361, 365 (1979). Compare Joseph Kupfer's defense of privacy as a necessary condition of autonomy, in particular the development of an autonomous self, in his "Privacy, Autonomy, and Self-Concept," *American Philosophical Quarterly* 24, 1 (1987), 81–89.

[33] Michael Sandel argues that the tendancy to identify privacy and autonomy is worrisome for another reason: namely, it obscures the shifting understandings of privacy in the law. See his *Democracy's Discontent: America in Search of a Public Philosophy* (Cambridge: Harvard University Press, 1996), 93.

[34] E.g., *Galella v. Onassis*, 487 F.2d 986 (2d Cir. 1978).

[35] E.g., *Dietemann v. Time, Inc.*, 449 F.2d 246 (9th Cir. 1971).

[36] E.g. *Whalen v. Roe*.

[37] *Dietemann v. Time, Inc.*, and *Galella v. Onassis* show how close privacy law is to harassment and trespass law. See also *Souder v. Pendleton Detectives*, 88 So. 2d 716 (La. App. 1956), and *Vogel v. W. T. Grant Co.*, 458 Pa. 124, 327 A.2d 133 (1974).

[38] Parent, "Privacy, Morality, and the Law," 273–274, 284. See also Parent, "A New Definition of Privacy," 316.

[39] See, for example, Gross, "Privacy and Autonomy," 180–181, as well as Henkin, "Privacy and Autonomy," discussed above.

[40] *Adkins v. Children's Hospital*, 261 U.S. 525 (1925). The cases are often referred to as the "Lochner era" after the first case, *Lochner v. New York*, 191 U.S. 45 (1905), which limited work hours in a bakery.

41 Some commentators and a few Supreme Court justices believe that under the name "privacy" the Court protected fundamental rights using
substantive due process, even if the justices did not admit it. See Gerald
Gunther, *Cases and Materials on Constitutional Law* (Mineola, N.Y.: Foundation Press, 1980), 502–503, 570–571; Justice Stewart in his comments
on *Griswold* and his concurrence in *Roe*; William Rehnquist, "Is an Expanded Right of Privacy Consistent with Fair and Consistent Law Enforcement? or Privacy, You've Come a Long Way, Baby," 23 *Kansas Law
Review* 1 (1974). Kenneth Winston has suggested an alternative interpretation to me, namely that the Court treated "privacy" as a component
of liberty, so that "liberty" is being used. But then there are ways (more
or less plausible) of distinguishing the privacy cases from the substantive
due process cases of earlier decades, even though "liberty" is at stake in
both.

42 State statutes have banned burning the flag as desecration, but in *Texas v.
Johnson*, 491 U.S. 397 (1989), the Supreme Court majority regarded burn-
ing the flag during a protest to be "expressive conduct" protected by the
First Amendment.

43 Ely, "The Wages of Crying Wolf," 932–933.

44 John Stuart Mill, *On Liberty* (New York: Penguin, 1976), 71. Compare the
ambiguous uses of the terms "private morality," "liberty," and "freedom
of choice and action" in the Hart-Devlin debate over legislation concerning homosexuality and prostitution. Patrick Devlin, "Morals and the Criminal Law," in *The Enforcement of Morals* (Oxford: Oxford University Press,
1965); H. L. A. Hart, "Immorality and Treason," *The Listener*, July 1959,
162–163.

45 Mill, *On Liberty*, 72. His interpretation here differs from the common Ar-
istotelian view of the relation between public and private given in chapter
1.

46 *Paris Adult Theatre I v. Slaton*, 413 U.S. 49 (1973). I thank Leslie Burkholder
for reminding me of this argument. There is also no evidence that the
Griswold Court viewed the privacy right as equivalent to a Mill-like right.

47 See the familiar account of moral autonomy sketched by Robert Paul Wolff
in his *In Defense of Anarchism* (New York: Harper and Row, 1970), 12–18.
Another defense of the view that the concepts of privacy and liberty are
intimately connected, although the terms have different meanings, is given
in Jeffrey L. Johnson, "Privacy, Liberty, and Integrity," *Public Affairs Quarterly* 3, 3 (1989), 15–34.

3. Definitions of Privacy, Philosophical Responses, and Conceptual Alternatives

1 Laurence H. Tribe, *American Constitutional Law*, 2d ed. (Mineola, N.Y.:
Foundation Press, 1988), 1303, describing Judith Jarvis Thomson, "The

Right to Privacy," *Philosophy and Public Affairs* 4 (1975), 295-314, especially 308-313, reprinted in Ferdinand David Schoeman, ed., *Philosophical Dimensions of Privacy: An Anthology* (Cambridge: Cambridge University Press, 1984), 272-289. For a critique of Thomson's essay, see Julie Inness, *Privacy, Intimacy, and Isolation* (Oxford: Oxford University Press, 1992), chap. 3.

2 Thomas Scanlon, "Thomson on Privacy," *Philosophy and Public Affairs* 4 (1975), 315-322; Jeffrey Reiman, "Privacy, Intimacy, and Personhood," *Philosophy and Public Affairs* 6 (1976), 26-44, reprinted in Schoeman, ed., *Philosophical Dimensions of Privacy*, 300-316. For William Parent, see chapter 2.

3 Janlori Goldman, statement before the Subcommittee on Technology and the Law, Committee on the Judiciary, U.S. Senate (August 1, 1990), reprinted in M. Ethan Katsh, ed., *Taking Sides: Clashing Views on Controversial Legal Issues*, 5th ed. (Guilford, Conn.: Dushkin, 1993), 335.

4 *Oxford English Dictionary* (Oxford: Clarendon Press, 1961), s.v. "private," *a.* 3.

5 In *Secrets: On the Ethics of Concealment and Revelation* (New York: Random House, Vintage Books, 1983), Sissela Bok discusses the complex relationships between privacy and secrecy. She suggests that often secrecy is used to guard what is private (see esp. 10-14). Kim Lane Scheppele's *Legal Secrets* (Chicago: University of Chicago Press, 1988) also addresses links between privacy and secrecy. Scheppele criticizes the economic theory of law analysis of privacy defended by Richard Posner in *The Economics of Justice* (Cambridge: Harvard University Press, 1981). She acknowledges that his theory may successfully explain some individual cases but argues that it does not provide an adequate account of the central features of the law of privacy and secrecy. Scheppele's alternative to the efficiency principle is an equality principle influenced by the social contract perspective and John Rawls's *Theory of Justice* (Cambridge: Harvard University Press, 1971).

6 The importance of this point should not be underestimated. John Hart Ely has claimed that privacy is not at stake in the constitutional abortion cases because abortions are performed in public, in the sense that others such as doctors and nurses are present. This claim presupposes that secrecy or concealment is at least a necessary condition of privacy, which I have just argued is false. See the discussion of Ely's argument in chapter 6.

7 Frederick Davis, "What Do We Mean By 'Right to Privacy'?" 4 *South Dakota Law Review* 1, 6 (1959).

8 *Pearson v. Dodd*, 410 F.2d 701 (D.C. Cir. 1969).

9 *Nader v. General Motors Corporation*, 25 N.Y.2d 560 (1970).

10 *Dietemann v. Time, Inc.*, 449 F.2d 246 (9th Cir. 1971).

11 Compare Thomson, "The Right to Privacy": "it seems to me none of us

has a right over any fact to the effect that that fact shall not be known to others." Yet "we have a right that certain steps shall not be taken to find out facts, and we have a right that certain uses shall not be made of facts" (307).

[12] Flora Colao and Tamar Hosansky, "The Key to Having Fun Is Being SAFE: Teaching Personal Safety to Children" (The Safety and Fitness Exchange, 1123 Broadway, N.Y., N.Y., 10010, n.d.).

[13] *Roe v. Wade*, 410 U.S. 113, 153–154 (1973).

[14] Ernst van den Haag, "On Privacy," in J. Roland Pennock and John W. Chapman, eds., *Privacy*, Nomos 13 (New York: Atherton Press, 1971), 149–168, esp. 150; Ruth Gavison, "Privacy and the Limits of Law," 89 *Yale Law Journal* 421 (1980), reprinted in Schoeman, ed., *Philosophical Dimensions of Privacy*, 346–402.

[15] Richard B. Parker, "A Definition of Privacy," 27 *Rutgers Law Review* 275, 279 (1974).

[16] van den Haag, "On Privacy." Thomas Scanlon claims that Thomson overstates the importance of property and ownership. Her examples, however, suggest that privacy rights can only sometimes be explained in terms of property rights; she argues they are at times derivative from a variety of other rights as well. It has been argued that many of the Fourth and Fifth Amendment cases, such as *Boyd v. United States*, 116 U.S. 616 (1886), *Weeks v. United States*, 232 U.S. 383 (1914), and *Gould v. United States*, 255 U.S. 298 (1921)—putting private papers beyond the reach of governmental agents, requiring warrants, and reaffirming the protection against self-incrimination—rest on traditional property concepts. See "Formalism, Legal Realism, and Constitutionally Protected Privacy under the Fourth and Fifth Amendments," 90 *Harvard Law Review* 945 (1977).

[17] Jeffrey H. Reiman, "Driving to the Panopticon: A Philosophical Exploration of the Risks to Privacy Posed by the Highway Technology of the Future," 11 *Santa Clara Computer and High Technology Law Journal* 27, 31–32 (1995).

[18] *Oxford English Dictionary*, s.v. "private," *a.* 7.

[19] See also Ferdinand Schoeman, "Privacy and Intimate Information," in Schoeman, ed., *Philosophical Dimensions of Privacy*, 403–418. Others who have emphasized intimacy as the core of privacy include Charles Fried, *An Anatomy of Values* (Cambridge: Harvard University Press, 1970), esp. 140, and Robert Gerstein, "Intimacy and Privacy," *Ethics* 89 (1978), 76–81, reprinted in Schoeman, ed., *Philosophical Dimensions of Privacy*, 265–271.

[20] Joel Feinberg, "Pornography and the Criminal Law," 40 *University of Pittsburgh Law Review* 567, 580 (1979). For a related view see Jeffrey L. Johnson, "Privacy and the Judgment of Others," *Journal of Value Inquiry* 23 (1989), 157–168, and "A Theory of the Nature and Value of Privacy," *Public Affairs Quarterly* 6, 3 (1992), 271–288.

21 This principle is the subject of Locke's first letter of toleration (1689), *A Letter Concerning Toleration* (Indianapolis: Bobbs-Merrill, 1955).

22 I am grateful to Jonathan Pressler for emphasizing the importance of this third problem.

23 William Parent, "Privacy, Morality, and the Law," *Philosophy and Public Affairs* 12 (1983), 278.

24 Harry Kalven, Jr., "Privacy in Tort Law—Were Warren and Brandeis Wrong?" *Law and Contemporary Problems* 31 (1966), 326–341. Richard Epstein has argued that privacy is the least important tort in "Privacy, Property Rights, and Misrepresentations," 12 *Georgia Law Review* 455 (1978). But the expanded protection of privacy in tort law is not as trivial as the original Warren and Brandeis protection.

25 Richard Posner, "The Right to Privacy," 12 *Georgia Law Review* 393 (1978).

26 Kim Lane Scheppele, "The Reasonable Woman," *Responsive Community, Rights, and Responsibilities,* 1, 4 (1991), 36–47, reprinted in abridged form in Joel Feinberg and Hyman Gross, eds., *Philosophy of Law,* 5th ed. (Belmont, Calif.: Wadsworth, 1995), 455.

27 Ibid., 453. Scheppele's is one of a number of discussions in literature concerning feminist jurisprudence and critical race studies on the importance of incorporating into law a commitment to understanding different points of view. See also Martha Minow, *Making All the Difference: Inclusion, Exclusion, and American Law* (Ithaca: Cornell University Press, 1990).

28 *Ellison v. Brady,* 924 F.2d 872 (9th Cir. 1991), *Robinson v. Jacksonville Shipyards,* 760 F. Supp. 1486 (M.D.Fla. 1991), and *Yates v. Avco Corp.,* 819 F.2d 630 (6th Cir. 1987).

29 As Scheppele points out, seeing the harm from the point of view of the class explicitly protected by a statute is not a radical move in civil cases. And in criminal cases with women defendants, *mens rea* (guilty mind) is determined from the point of view of the *particular defendant.* Asking a court to see the criminal nature of the defendant's conduct as dependent on the *victim's* point of view, as in consent for rape cases, is a more radical departure. Yet it may well be justifiable. For example, fleeing in a dangerous and unfamiliar city neighborhood at two o'clock in the morning may seem feasible to a reasonable man but may not appear to a woman to be a reasonable choice or option.

4. Defending a Broad Conception of Privacy

1 *Whalen v. Roe,* 429 U.S. 589, 599, 600 (1977).

2 As representatives of these different views, Tribe cites respectively Judith Jarvis Thomson, "The Right to Privacy," *Philosophy and Public Affairs* 4 (1975), 295–314; Jeffrey Reiman, "Privacy, Intimacy and Personhood," *Philosophy and Public Affairs* 6 (1976), 26–44, and Ruth Gavison, "Privacy

and the Limits of Law," 89 *Yale Law Journal* 421 (1980). All are reprinted in Ferdinand David Schoeman, ed., *Philosphical Dimensions of Privacy: An Anthology* (Cambridge: Cambridge University Press, 1984), 272–289, 300–316, 346–402.

3   Laurence H. Tribe, *American Constitutional Law*, 2d ed. (Mineola, N.Y.: Foundation Press, 1988), 1303.

4   Ibid., 1304.

5   Ronald Dworkin, "What Is Equality? Part I: Equality of Welfare," *Philosophy and Public Affairs* 10, 3 (1981), 185.

6   Tribe, *American Constitutional Law*, 1389–1390.

7   William Rehnquist, "Is an Expanded Right of Privacy Consistent with Fair and Consistent Law Enforcement? or Privacy, You've Come a Long Way, Baby," 23 *Kansas Law Review* 1 (1974).

8   *Union Pacific Railway v. Botsford*, 141 U.S. 251–252 (1891). *Botsford* was overruled because of its incompatibility with new civil procedure rules in *Sibbach v. Wilson and Company, Inc.*, 312 U.S. 1 (1940), over a vigorous dissent by Justice Frankfurter, joined by Justices Black, Douglas, and Murphy.

9   Ferdinand Schoeman, *Privacy and Social Freedom* (Cambridge: Cambridge University Press, 1992), 2. Hereafter cited parenthetically in the text. For a related discussion see Jeffrey L. Johnson, "Constitutional Privacy," *Law and Philosophy* 13 (1994), 161–193.

10   Jeffrey Reiman makes a similar claim in somewhat more general words: "I can sum up that value [of privacy] as: the protection of freedom, moral personality, and a rich and critical inner life." See "Driving to the Panopticon: A Philosophical Exploration of the Risks to Privacy Posed by the Highway Technology of the Future," 11 *Santa Clara Computer and High Technology Law Journal* 27, 42 (1995).

11   An explicit defense of this definition of privacy appears in Charles Fried's *An Anatomy of Values* (Cambridge: Harvard University Press, 1970), 140.

12   Alan Westin, *Privacy and Freedom* (New York: Atheneum Press: 1967), 7.

13   Gavison, "Privacy and the Limits of Law," 428.

14   Compare Michael Sandel, *Democracy's Discontent: America in Search of a Public Philosophy* (Cambridge: Harvard University Press, 1996), chap. 4, esp. 105, as well as *Planned Parenthood v. Casey*, 505 U.S. 833; 112 S. Ct. 2791, 2807 (1992), where privacy is said to protect "the most intimate and personal choices a person may make in a lifetime, choices central to personal dignity and autonomy" and "the right to define one's own concept of existence." See also Robert S. Gerstein, "California's Constitutional Right to Privacy: The Development of the Protection of Private Life," 9 *Hastings Constitutional Law Quarterly* 385 (1982), and Joseph Kupfer, "Privacy, Autonomy, and Self-Concept," *American Philosophical Quarterly* 24, 1 (1987), 81–89.

15   Gavison, "Privacy and the Limits of Law," 448.

16 Tom Gerety, "Redefining Privacy," 12 *Harvard Civil Rights–Civil Liberties Law Review* 233, 236 (1977).
17 These cases are discussed in chapter 1, with nn. 40, 44–47, 49.
18 See the discussion of this point in Ronald Dworkin, *Life's Dominion: An Argument about Abortion, Euthanasia, and Individual Freedom* (New York: Knopf, 1993).
19 Michael Martin, *The Legal Philosophy of H. L. A. Hart: A Critical Appraisal* (Philadelphia: Temple University Press, 1987), 52–53.
20 Others are working on this task. See, for example, Laurence H. Tribe and Michael C. Dorf, *On Reading the Constitution* (Cambridge: Harvard University Press, 1991), for a constitutional defense of unenumerated rights. They provide a constitutional defense of privacy based on generalizing protection of peaceful assembly from the First Amendment and special (though not absolute) solicitude for the home in the Third Amendment, as well as Fourth Amendment protection (59–60, 116–117). See also David A. J. Richards, "Constitutional Privacy, Religious Disestablishment, and the Abortion Decisions," in Jay Garfield and Patricia Hennessey, eds., *Abortion: Moral and Legal Perspectives* (Amherst: University of Massachusetts Press, 1984), 148–174.

5. The Feminist Critique of Privacy

1 Tom Gerety, "Redefining Privacy," 12 *Harvard Civil Rights–Civil Liberties Law Review* 233, 236 (1977).
2 Catharine MacKinnon, *Toward a Feminist Theory of the State* (Cambridge: Harvard University Press, 1989), 187. In this passage, she cites Kenneth I. Karst, "The Freedom of Intimate Association," 89 *Yale Law Journal* 624 (1980); Tom Grey, "Eros, Civilization, and the Burger Court," 43 *Law and Contemporary Problems* 83 (1980); and others.
3 *Whalen v. Roe*, 429 U.S. 589, 599, 600 (1977).
4 For example, see Louis Henkin, "Privacy and Autonomy," 74 *Columbia Law Review* 1410 (1974), and Hyman Gross, "The Concept of Privacy," 42 *New York Law Review* 34 (1967) on the separation of the interests. See also Judith Wagner DeCew, "The Scope of Privacy in Law and Ethics," *Law and Philosophy* 5 (1986), 145–173, on connections between them. Others who take this latter view include Ferdinand Schoeman, *Privacy and Social Freedom* (Cambridge: Cambridge University Press, 1992) and Julie Inness, *Privacy, Intimacy, and Isolation* (Oxford: Oxford University Press, 1992).
5 MacKinnon, *Toward a Feminist Theory of the State*, 164–165.
6 Ibid., 191.
7 The old rape shield laws, for example, made it impossible for women to claim their husbands had raped them.
8 See chapter 2 and William Parent, "Privacy, Morality, and the Law," *Phi-*

losophy and Public Affairs 12 (1983), 269–288, for examples and discussion of this point.

9 See Carole Pateman, "Feminist Critiques of the Public/Private Dichotomy," in *The Disorder of Women: Democracy, Feminism, and Political Theory* (Stanford: Stanford University Press, 1989), 127, for example, on enfranchising women.

10 Ibid., 118. Also quoted in Susan Moller Okin, *Justice, Gender, and the Family* (New York: Basic Books, 1989), 111.

11 See Ruth Gavison, "Feminism and the Public/Private Distinction," 45 *Stanford Law Review* 1 (1992). She reviews and carefully assesses many different interpretations of the feminist critique of the public/private distinction.

12 As Melinda Roberts has pointed out to me, if rights such as the right to leave one's husband *were* enforced legally and effectively, the state *would* be intruding into a private domain and would in this sense be "exploding" the private.

13 MacKinnon, *Toward a Feminist Theory of the State*, 190; see also 205. Okin, *Justice, Gender, and the Family*, has made the reverse point, that injustice at home is necessarily mirrored in public.

14 Jean Bethke Elshtain, *Democracy on Trial* (New York: Basic Books, 1995), 43.

Gavison, "Feminism and the Public/Private Distinction," 28, 28–29.

16 Another who seems to endorse this view is Supreme Court Justice Ruth Bader Ginsberg, "Some Thoughts on Autonomy and Equality in Relation to *Roe v. Wade*," 63 *North Carolina Law Review* 375 (1985). See also Kenneth L. Karst, "Foreword: Equal Citizenship under the Fourteenth Amendment," 91 *Harvard Law Review* 1 (1977). For replies to this approach, see Gavison, "Feminism and the Public/Private Distinction," 31–35.

17 Anita Allen, *Uneasy Access: Privacy for Women in a Free Society* (Totowa, N.J.: Rowman and Littlefield, 1988), 40. But see my review of her book in *Philosophical Review* 101 (1992), 709–711, describing why this reply is incomplete.

18 Okin, *Justice, Gender, and the Family*, 174. See also MacKinnon, *Toward a Feminist Theory of the State*, 244.

19 MacKinnon, *Toward a Feminist Theory of the State*, 194.

20 See, for example, Frances Olsen, "The Myth of State Intervention in the Family," 18 *University of Michigan Journal of Law Reform* 835 (1985), for an explanation of the government's pervasive involvement in black women's lives. I am grateful to Barbara Schulman for stressing this distinction.

21 Jean Bethke Elshtain's critique of this feminist view is related to my own yet differs in that it is based on political considerations. Calling attention to a serious problem that puts democracy on trial, she writes, "if there are no distinctions between public and private, personal and political, it fol-

lows that there can be no differentiated activity or set of institutions that are genuinely political, the purview of citizens and the bases of order, legitimacy, and purpose in a democratic community" (*Democracy on Trial*, 44).

22　See the proceedings of Changing Perspectives of the Family, a symposium held April 16, 1994, at the Constitutional Law Resource Center at Drake University, Des Moines, Iowa, for a contemporary discussion of the implications of changing perspectives of the family in both constitutional law and family law and for a discussion of the degree to which the state may organize and control intimate relationships.

23　I am indebted to Joan Callahan for emphasizing the importance of this interpretation.

24　Frances E. Olsen, "The Family and the Market: A Study of Ideology and Legal Reform," 96 *Harvard Law Review* 1497 (1983), reprinted in Patricia Smith, ed., *Feminist Jurisprudence* (Oxford: Oxford University Press, 1993), 65–93; quote at 68. Hereafter cited parenthetically in the text.

25　Pateman, "Feminist Critiques," 120.

26　Ibid., 121–122, 123.

27　John Stuart Mill, *The Subjection of Women* (1869; reprint, Indianapolis: Hackett, 1988).

28　Pateman, "Feminist Critiques," 133.

29　I owe this point to Diana Meyers. She has suggested that the debate over privacy may have an important pragmatic dimension as well. Those who believe the battery of women is so pervasive, and the need to expose it to stop the abuse so urgent, that it almost always compromises women's autonomy (whether women acknowledge that or not) will be drawn to MacKinnon's full-blown critique of privacy. Those who believe domestic violence, despite its severity, can be addressed without giving up the value of privacy will be attracted to a more moderate approach.

6. Judicial Interpretation and John Hart Ely's Critique of *Roe v. Wade*

1　*Roe v. Wade*, 410 U.S. 113 (1973).

2　John Hart Ely, "The Wages of Crying Wolf: A Comment on *Roe v. Wade*," 82 *Yale Law Journal* 920 (1973).

3　Paul Brest, "The Misconceived Quest for the Original Understanding," 60 *Boston University Law Review* 204, 204 (1980). See also Earl M. Maltz, *Rethinking Constitutional Law: Originalism, Interventionism, and the Politics of Judicial Review* (Lawrence: University Press of Kansas, 1984).

4　Edwin Meese, "Construing the Constitution," 19 *University of California at Davis Law Review* 22 (1985).

5　See Brest, "The Misconceived Quest."

6　Robert Bork, "Neutral Principles and Some First Amendment Problems," 47 *Indiana Law Journal* 1 (1971); Raoul Berger, *Government by the Judiciary*

(Cambridge: Harvard University Press, 1977); Henry Monaghan, "Our Perfect Constitution," 56 *New York University Law Review* 353 (1981).

7   Theodore Benditt, *Law as Rule and Principle* (Brighton, Sussex: Harvester Press, 1978). See also Judith Wagner DeCew, "Realities about Legal Realism," *Law and Philosophy* 4 (1985), 405–422.

8   With characteristic vision, Lon Fuller charged that "our courts' piece-meal and backward-looking system of legislating frequently proves inadequate to meet the need for legal control in fields where social practices are changing rapidly"; "American Legal Realism," 82 *University of Pennsylvania Law Review* 439 (1934), quoted in Kenneth I. Winston, "Is/Ought Redux: The Pragmatist Context of Lon Fuller's Conception of Law," 8 *Oxford Journal of Legal Studies* 329, 331n (1988).

9   Ronald Dworkin, *Taking Rights Seriously* (Cambridge: Harvard University Press, 1977), and *Law's Empire* (Cambridge: Harvard University Press, 1986).

10 Alexander Bickel, *The Least Dangerous Branch* (New York: Bobbs-Merrill, 1962); Brest, "The Misguided Quest," 205.

11 John Hart Ely, *Democracy and Distrust: A Theory of Judicial Review* (Cambridge: Harvard University Press, 1980).

12 Thomas B. Stoddard, "*Bowers v. Hardwick*: Precedent by Personal Predilection," 54 *University of Chicago Law Review* 648, 648 (1987).

13 *Roe v. Wade*, 410 U.S. 113, 159 (1973).

14 Idem at 162.

15 Ely, "The Wages of Crying Wolf," 923. Hereafter cited parenthetically in the text.

16 Compare Judith Jarvis Thomson's assumption that a fetus *is* a person and subsequent argument defending abortion even given that assumption. See "A Defense of Abortion," *Philosophy and Public Affairs* 4 (1975), 295–314.

17 Ian Shapiro, ed., *Abortion: The Supreme Court Decisions* (Cambridge, Mass.: Hackett, 1995), 14; Ronald Dworkin, *Life's Dominion* (New York: Knopf, 1993), 107.

18 Consider, for example, that some intrauterine devices and many popular birth control pills either fail to prevent fertilization or destroy fertilized ova.

19 *United States v. Carolene Products*, 304 U.S. 144, 152 n. 4 (1938).

20 See chapter 2.

21 Alexander Bickel, *The Supreme Court and the Idea of Progress* (New York: Harper and Row, 1970), 177. See also Hans A. Linde, "Judges, Critics, and the Realist Tradition," 82 *Yale Law Journal* 227, 233–235 (1972).

22 Ronald Dworkin, *Taking Rights Seriously*; *A Matter of Principle* (Cambridge: Harvard University Press, 1985); *Law's Empire*.

23 Ely, *Democracy and Distrust*, 100–101.

24 Harm construed as ending the potential for viability is another question, of course, but the harm Ely has alluded to in discussing other cases appears to be sensed harm.
25 *Webster v. Reproductive Health Services,* 492 U.S. 490 (1989). See Judith Wagner DeCew, "Threatening Constitutional Protection for Abortion," *Radcliffe Quarterly* 74, 4 (1989), 6–9.
26 *United States v. Vuitch,* 402 U.S. 62, 80 (1971).

7. Constitutional Privacy and the Arguments in *Bowers v. Hardwick*

1 *Bowers v. Hardwick,* 478 U.S. 186 (1986), hereafter cited parenthetically in the text. Compare related arguments on privacy and sodomy in Richard A. Mohr's *Gays/Justice* (New York: Columbia University Press, 1988).
2 *Georgia Code Ann.* section 16-6-2 (1984).
3 Laurence H. Tribe, *American Constitutional Law,* 2d ed. (Mineola, N.Y.: Foundation Press, 1988), 1428. See also Laurence H. Tribe and Michael C. Dorf, *On Reading the Constitution* (Cambridge: Harvard University Press, 1991), esp. 74–76, and Michael Sandel, *Democracy's Discontent: America in Search of a Public Philosophy* (Cambridge: Harvard University Press, 1996), 107, for further comparison of the questions asked by the majority and minority.
4 Joseph R. Thornton, "*Bowers v. Hardwick*: An Incomplete Constitutional Analysis," 65 *North Carolina Law Review* 1101 (1987).
5 *Eisenstadt v. Baird,* 405 U.S. 438 (1972).
6 *Carey v. Population Services International,* 431 U.S. 678 (1977).
7 Tribe and Dorf, *On Reading the Constitution,* 58.
8 Tribe and Dorf conclude, "This seems like the wrong way to go about developing principles of privacy" (ibid., 58). But the majority, of course, denies privacy is even relevant to the case. For a constitutional justification of unenumerated rights such as privacy, see the discussion in Tribe and Dorf, 59ff.
9 478 U.S. at 205, citing *Paris Adult Theatre I v. Slaton,* 413 U.S. 49, 63 (1973).
10 Stuart Hampshire, *Morality and Conflict* (Cambridge: Harvard University Press, 1983), 153.
11 *Stanley v. Georgia,* 394 U.S. 557 (1969).
12 *Cammermeyer v. Aspin,* 850 F. Supp. 910 (W.D.Wash. 1994).
13 *Griswold v. Connecticut,* 381 U.S. 479, 530 (1965) (Stewart, J., dissenting).
14 Hampshire, *Morality and Conflict,* 137.
15 Patrick Devlin, "Morals and the Criminal Law," in *The Enforcement of Morals* (Oxford: Oxford University Press, 1965); H. L. A. Hart, "Immorality and Treason," *The Listener,* July 1959, 162–163.
16 See Ronald Dworkin, *Taking Rights Seriously* (Cambridge: Harvard University Press, 1977), 242.
17 John Stuart Mill, *On Liberty* (New York: Penguin, 1976), 68.

18 On this last point see also Dworkin, *Taking Rights Seriously*, 255.

19 See chapter 6.

20 *San Antonio Independent School District v. Rodriguez*, 411 U.S. 1 (1973) (on school financing systems).

21 *Matthews v. Lucas*, 427 U.S. 495 (1976) (on illegitimate children).

22 *Rodriguez*.

23 *Rodriguez* and *United States v. Carolene Products*, 304 U.S. 144 (1938).

24 For example, in 1988 a panel of judges of the U.S. Ninth Circuit Court of Appeals in California ordered openly gay Sergeant Perry Watkins reinstated in the U.S. Army. His lawyers won by relying on showing unjust discrimination against the class of gays and distinguished this case on the grounds that it only involved professed sexual orientation, no charge of a specific act of sodomy (William A. Henry III, "Uniform Treatment for Gays," *Time*, February 22, 1988, 55). The New York Court of Appeals expressly extended constitutional protection to homosexual conduct in *People v. Onofre*, 51 N.Y.2d 476, 485 (1980), *cert. denied*, 451 U.S. 987 (1981), but this is the overwhelming exception.

25 In 1993 the Hawaii Supreme Court remanded the case for trial leading to Chang's ruling. *Baehr v. Miike*, Cir. Ct. of the First District, State of Hawaii, Civ. No. 91-1394-05.

26 Compare Thornton, "*Bowers v. Hardwick*," 1122.

27 Thomas B. Stoddard, "*Bowers v. Hardwick*: Precedent by Personal Predilection," 54 *University of Chicago Law Review* 648 (1987).

28 Mitchell L. Pearl, "Chipping Away at *Bowers v. Hardwick*: Making the Best of an Unfortunate Decision," 63 *New York University Law Review* 154 (1988).

29 Tribe, *American Constitutional Law*, 1431.

30 See Julia K. Sullens, "Thus Far and No Further: The Supreme Court Draws the Outer Boundary of the Right to Privacy," 61 *Tulane Law Review* 907 (1987).

31 Daniel J. Langin, "*Bowers v. Hardwick*: The Right of Privacy and the Question of Intimate Relations," 70 *Iowa Law Review* 1443 (1987).

8. Drug Testing: A Case Study in Balancing Privacy and Public Safety

1 For discussions of a variety of questions related to HIV and privacy, see the papers in Daniel Wueste, ed., *AIDS: Crisis in Professional Ethics* (Philadelphia: Temple University Press, 1994). For a discussion focused on HIV and testing issues, see Martin Gunderson, David J. Mayo, and Frank S. Rhame, *AIDS: Testing and Privacy* (Salt Lake City: University of Utah Press, 1989).

2 See, for example, the data cited in Michael R. O'Donnell, "Employee Drug Testing—Balancing the Interests in the Workplace: A Reasonable Suspicion," 74 *Virginia Law Review* 969, 971, 972 (1988).

3 Nancy Perkins, "Prohibiting the Use of the Human Immunodeficiency

Virus Antibody Test by Employers and Insurers," *Harvard Journal of Legislation* 25 (1988), 297–303.

4 Cathryn Jo Rosen and John S. Goldkamp, "The Constitutionality of Drug Testing at the Bail Stage," 80 *Journal of Criminal Law and Criminology* 114, 117 (1989).

5 Edward S. Adams, "Random Drug Testing of Government Employees: A Constitutional Procedure," 54 *University of Chicago Law Review*, 1335, 1337 (1988), quoting Thomas E. Geidt, "Drug and Alcohol Abuse in the Work Place: Balancing Employer and Employee Rights," 11 *Employee Relations Law Journal* 181, 184 (1986).

6 John Horgan, "Test Negative," *Scientific American*, March 1990, 18.

7 Adams, "Random Drug Testing," 1337. Steven Wisotsky claims that testing is practiced at as many as 80 percent of Fortune 500 companies, in "A Society of Suspects: The War on Drugs and Civil Liberties," *Policy Analysis* 180 (1992), 12. The percentage is even higher according to a 1995 Research Survey of Privacy in the Workplace by David Linowes, University of Illinois at Urbana-Champaign. For an in-depth discussion of employee drug testing and privacy, see John Gilliom, *Surveillance, Privacy, and the Law: Employee Drug Testing and the Politics of Social Control* (Ann Arbor: University of Michigan Press, 1996).

8 See Matthew Finkin, *Privacy in Employment Law* (Washington, D.C.: BNA Books, 1995), chap 2.

9 Horgan, "Test Negative," 18.

10 Alan R. Westin et al., "College and University Policies on Substance Abuse and Drug Testing," *Academe* 78, 3 (1992), 20.

11 As an indicator of accuracy, "sensitivity" indicates the ability of a test accurately to detect a specimen containing the drug, whereas "specificity" deals with the ability of a test accurately to detect specimens that do not contain the drug. See Finkin, *Privacy in Employment Law*, 29.

12 Arthur J. McBay, "Drug-Analysis Technology—Pitfalls and Problems of Drug Testing," *Clinical Chemistry* 33, 11 (1987), 34B.

13 David J. Greenblatt and Richard I. Shader, "Say 'No' to Drug Testing," *Journal of Clinical Psychopharmocology* 10 (1990), 157.

14 McBay, "Drug-Analysis Technology," 34B.

15 A federal district court held that observation of the employee while the sample was given (but not including observation of the donor's genitals) was not constitutionally unreasonable. *Wilcher v. City of Wilmington*, 891 F. Supp. 993 (D. Del. 1995).

16 McBay, "Drug-Analysis Technology," 37B.

17 Greenblatt and Shader, "Say 'No' to Drug Testing," 157.

18 Arthur J. McBay, "Drugs and Transportation Safety," *Journal of Forensic Science* 35 (1990), 523.

19 Horgan, "Test Negative," 19. A recent and comprehensive study of drug

tests and what they reveal about usage is J. Normand, R. Lempert, and C.
O'Brien, eds., *Under the Influence: Drugs and the American Work Force*, National
Research Council/Institute of Medicine (Washington, D.C.; National
Academy Press, 1994).

[20] *National Treasury Employees Union v. Von Raab*, 489 U.S. 656 (1989); *Skinner
v. Railway Labor Executives' Association*, 489 U.S. 602 (1989).

[21] *Katz v. United States*, 389 U.S. 347, 361 (1967). Compare the discussion of
this case in chapter 1.

[22] *Vernonia School District 47J v. Acton*, 115 S. Ct. 2386 (1995). Acknowledging
the privacy interests involved, the Court nevertheless permitted the drug
testing in a 6–3 decision. In addition to evidence of drug use by athletes
at school, the Court noted the test method that allowed monitors in the
bathroom but not direct observation, as well as the safeguards in place for
protecting the test information. But the Court majority emphasized the
schools' custodial responsibility and concluded, "We caution against the
assumption that suspicionless drug testing will readily pass consitutional
muster in other contexts" (2396). The Supreme Court has granted cer-
tiori in a more interesting case on the question whether the state of Georgia can require drug tests for candidates for public office, *Chandler v. Miller*,
73 F.3d 1543 (11th Cir. 1996). The decision, expected in 1997, will presumably address privacy concerns as well as implications of the worry that
those opposed to such drug tests will be deterred from running for office.

[23] The analogy is from Phyllis T. Bookspan, "Jar Wars: Employee Drug Testing, the Constitution, and the American Drug Problem," 26 *American Criminal Law Review* 359, 388 (1988).

[24] Matthew Finkin pointed out to me that in the private sector, four states
limit applicant screening to safety-sensitive jobs by judicial decision (Mass.,
N.J., W.Va.) or by statute (Mont.), and ten require a confirmatory GC/MS
test after a positive screen. But most state courts have no problem dis-
charging an employee after years of satisfactory service from a job that is
not safety sensitive because of refusal to take a test (e.g., *Gilmore v. Enogex*,
878 P.2d 360 [Okla. 1994]) or because of a positive test (*Seta v. Reading
Rock*, 654 N.E. 2d 1061 [Ohio App. 1995]).

[25] Some do believe the problems with drug testing are extensive enough that
no drug testing can be justified, urging it is preferable to use a straightforward competence criterion. I do not defend this absolute view.

[26] Justice Scalia wrote a dissenting opinion in *Von Raab*. One could claim that
the Supreme Court majority was merely arguing that such testing is not
unconstitutional and was withholding judgment on the wisdom of the policy. But my reading of the opinion indicates the Court endorsed both
positions.

[27] Such programs might include impairment testing in lieu of more invasive
drug testing.

[28] It has been suggested to me that some would prefer random testing to testing based on "reasonable suspicion," since in the former case the test would not seem aimed at them personally. But the possibility of such a preference does not outweigh the moral, political, and economic arguments against random testing. See the arguments in *Vernonia School District 47J v. Acton.*

[29] In such cases it might be argued that if an employee consents to take a job knowing she will be tested for drugs, then she does not have a complaint. But as Hilde Nelson has pointed out to me, this suggests that consent is all that is morally relevant in the interaction between employee and employer, and the situation is usually more complicated. If what the employee has consented to is clearly unjust, she is blameworthy for having given consent. If the prospective employee does not have several job offers to choose from, her consent is not free. Even if she does have other jobs to choose from, her choosing this job over the others because she finds it the most attractive does not mean that she consents to all features of the job: she might find one or two of them morally problematic and hope to change them in the course of her work. Matthew Finkin has shown that on the issue of consent some courts have applied a Catch-22: if an employee refuses to test (and is fired) there was no invasion of privacy; if an employee tests positive (and is fired) he consented, thus precluding a subsequent claim of an invasion of privacy (*Privacy in Employment Law*, 42–43).

9. Information Technology: A Challenge to Privacy Protection

[1] For a related view on the importance of privacy protection in the face of developing information technologies, see Jeffrey H. Reiman, "Driving to the Panopticon: A Philosophical Exploration of the Risks to Privacy Posed by the Highway Technology of the Future," 11 *Santa Clara Computer and High Technology Law Journal* 27 (1995).

[2] This case is described in an op-ed piece: Judith Wagner DeCew, "Your Privacy Is Being Threatened," *Philadelphia Inquirer*, February 23, 1991, widely reprinted in newspapers under various titles.

[3] Jeffrey Rothfeder, "Is Nothing Private?" *Business Week*, September 4, 1989, 81.

[4] Ibid., 74.

[5] Ibid.

[6] Michele Galen, "The Right to Privacy: There's More Loophole Than Law," *Business Week*, September 4, 1989, 77.

[7] Daniel Akst, "We Know Where You Live . . . ," *Boston Globe*, October 16, 1995, 11. Although the IRS is forbidden by law to disclose individual taxpayer returns, those of corporations and tax-exempt entities are matters of public record and could be available on-line.

8 Michael W. Miller, "Equifax to Stop Selling Its Data to Junk Mailers," *Wall Street Journal*, August 9, 1991, B1–B2.

9 Charles Piller, "Privacy in Peril," *MacWorld*, July 1993, 126.

10 Saul Hansell, "Keeping Identity Thieves at Bay," *New York Times*, June 16, 1996, sect. 4, 5.

11 John Markoff, "Europe's Plans to Protect Privacy Worry Business," *New York Times*, April 11, 1991, A1+; Larry Tye, "EC May Force New Look at Privacy," *Boston Globe*, September 7, 1993, 10. An excellent summary of the European approach is supplied in Paul M. Schwartz, "European Data Protection Law and Restrictions on International Data Flows," 80 *Iowa Law Review* 471 (1995). On the domestic approaches in Germany and Sweden, see Colin Bennett, *Regulating Privacy: Data Protection and Public Policy in Europe and the United States* (Ithaca: Cornell University Press, 1992). See also Charles Franklin, ed., *Business Guide to Privacy and Data Protection Legislation* (Dordrecht: Kluwer Law International, 1996), where the text of the Council of Europe OECD and national laws in Europe are summarized and explained, with relevant portions translated.

12 Larry Tye, "No Private Lives: German System Puts a Lid on Data," *Boston Globe*, September 7, 1993, 1+.

13 Ibid., 10.

14 Part of the following argument appeared in an op-ed piece as Judith Wagner DeCew, "Caller ID a Subtle Threat to Privacy," *Middlesex News* (Mass.), February 17, 1994, widely reprinted in newspapers under various titles.

15 Richard Lacayo, "Now We've Really Got Your Number," *Time*, November 11, 1991, 40.

16 Glenn Chatmas Smith, "We've Got Your Number! (Is It Constitutional to Give It Out?): Caller Identification Technology and the Right to Informational Privacy," 37 *U.C.L.A. Law Review* 145 (1989); Arthur Miller, statement before the Subcommittee on Technology and the Law, Committee on the Judiciary, U.S. Senate (August 1, 1990), reprinted in M. Ethan Katsh, ed., *Taking Sides: Clashing Views on Controversial Legal Issues*, 5th ed. (Guilford, Conn.: Dushkin, 1993), 342–344. Miller supports caller ID, arguing that the caller's claim to privacy is weak or nonexistent, whereas he favors allowing caller ID to protect the privacy of called parties, who have "the superior privacy right" (343).

17 *Smith v. Maryland* 442 U.S. 735, 747, 748 (1979). In this case the Court held that law enforcement officials do not need a search warrant to install a pen register, a device that records numbers dialed from a telephone. The majority wrote, "All telephone users realize that they must 'convey' phone numbers to the telephone company, since it is through telephone company switching equipment that their calls are completed. All subscribers realize, moreover, that the phone company has facilities for making permanent records of the numbers they dial" (442 U.S. at 742, cited in

Miller, statement, 343). The *Smith* court may not have anticipated and envisioned the further privacy problems of advanced telephone technology, as described later in this chapter.

[18] Attorney Janlori Goldman, speaking for the ACLU, statement before the Subcommittee on Technology and the Law, Committee on the Judiciary, U.S. Senate (August 1, 1990), reprinted in Katsh, ed., *Taking Sides*, 334–341.

[19] Ibid., 337.

[20] Richard Carelli, "Court Clears Baby Bells for Information Fields," *Boston Globe*, October 31, 1991, 53+. To the dismay of consumers and news and broadcasting groups, the Supreme Court, without comment, rejected a request to bar the Baby Bell companies from using telephone lines in this way.

[21] Barry Steinhardt is quoted in Charles Edward Anderson, "Night Callers Beware," *ABA Journal* 75 (May 1989), 30.

[22] Mary Lu Carnevale, "Caller ID Rings With New Controversies," *Wall Street Journal*, March 25, 1991, B1–B2.

[23] The term "dynamic negotiation" was introduced and the concept of a solution was developed by Ross E. Mitchell in Ross E. Mitchell and Judith Wagner DeCew, "Dynamic Negotiation in the Privacy Wars," *Technology Review* 97, 8 (1994), 70–71.

[24] Carnevale, "Caller ID Rings."

[25] Ronald Rosenberg, "New Service for Phones Will Tell Who's Calling," *Boston Globe*, October 14, 1992, 1+.

[26] Letter signed by Bailey Geeslin, *New York Times*, June 20, 1991, D23.

[27] Goldman, statement, 340. See also an editorial, "Phone Privacy—at a Price," *Boston Globe*, February 10, 1992, 14.

[28] *Barasch v. Pennsylvania Public Utility Commission*, 133 Pa. Commw. 285, 576 A.2d 79 (1990). The case is also discussed in Don J. Benedictis, "Caller ID on Hold," *ABA Journal* 76 (September 1990), 28.

[29] For discussions of various questions related to HIV and privacy, see the papers in Daniel Wueste, ed., *AIDS: Crisis in Professional Ethics* (Philadelphia: Temple University Press, 1994). For a discussion focused on HIV and testing issues, see Martin Gunderson, David J. Mayo, and Frank S. Rhame, *AIDS: Testing and Privacy* (Salt Lake City: University of Utah Press, 1989).

[30] Piller, "Privacy in Peril," 126.

Selected Bibliography

Allen, Anita. *Uneasy Access: Privacy for Women in a Free Society.* Totowa, N.J.: Rowman and Littlefield, 1988.

Benditt, Theodore. *Law as Rule and Principle.* [Brighton], Sussex: Harvester Press, 1978.

Benn, Stanley I,. and Gerald Gaus, eds. *The Private and Public in Social Policy.* London: Croon Helm; New York: St. Martin's Press, 1983.

Bennett, Colin. *Regulating Privacy: Data Protection and Public Policy in Europe and the United States.* Ithaca: Cornell University Press, 1992.

Berger, Raoul. *Government by the Judiciary.* Cambridge: Harvard University Press, 1977.

Berlin, Isaiah. *Four Essays on Liberty.* Oxford: Oxford University Press, 1969.

Bickel, Alexander. *The Least Dangerous Branch.* New York: Bobbs-Merrill, 1962.

——. *The Supreme Court and the Idea of Progress.* New York: Harper and Row, 1970.

Bok, Sissela. *Secrets: On the Ethics of Concealment and Revelation.* New York: Random House, Vintage Books, 1983.

Devlin, Patrick. *The Enforcement of Morals.* Oxford: Oxford University Press, 1965.

Dworkin, Ronald. *Law's Empire.* Cambridge: Harvard University Press, 1986.

——. *Life's Dominion: An Argument about Abortion, Euthanasia, and Individual Freedom.* New York: Knopf, 1993.

——. *A Matter of Principle.* Cambridge: Harvard University Press, 1985.

——. *Taking Rights Seriously.* Cambridge: Harvard University Press, 1977.

Elshtain, Jean Bethke. *Democracy on Trial.* New York: Basic Books, 1995.

——. *Public Man, Private Woman: Women in Social and Political Thought.* Princeton: Princeton University Press, 1981.

Ely, John Hart. *Democracy and Distrust: A Theory of Judicial Review.* Cambridge: Harvard University Press, 1980.

Feinberg, Joel. *Social Philosophy.* Englewood Cliffs, N.J.: Prentice-Hall, 1973.

Feinberg, Joel, and Hyman Gross. *Philosophy of Law.* 5th ed. Belmont, Calif.: Wadsworth, 1995.

Franklin, Charles, ed. *Business Guide to Privacy and Data Protection Legislation.* Dordrecht: Kluwer Law International, 1996.

Fried, Charles. *An Anatomy of Values.* Cambridge: Harvard University Press, 1970.

Garfield, Jay, and Patricia Hennessey, eds. *Abortion: Moral and Legal Perspectives.* Amherst: University of Massachusetts Press, 1984.

Gilliom, John. *Surveillance, Privacy, and the Law: Employee Drug Testing and the Politics of Social Control.* Ann Arbor: University of Michigan Press, 1996.

Gunderson, Martin, David J. Mayo, and Frank S. Rhame. *AIDS: Testing and Privacy.* Salt Lake City: University of Utah Press, 1989.

Gunther, Gerald. *Individual Rights in Constitutional Law.* Mineola, N.Y.: Foundation Press, 1986.

Hampshire, Stuart. *Morality and Conflict.* Cambridge: Harvard University Press, 1983.

Inness, Julie. *Privacy, Intimacy, and Isolation.* Oxford: Oxford University Press, 1992.

Jaggar, Alison, ed. *Living with Contradictions.* Boulder, Colo.: Westview Press, 1994.

Katsh, M. Ethan, ed. *Taking Sides: Clashing Views on Controversial Legal Issues.* 5th ed. Guilford, Conn.: Dushkin, 1993.

Kupfer, Joseph H. *Autonomy and Social Interaction.* Albany: State University of New York Press, 1990.

MacKinnon, Catharine. *Toward a Feminist Theory of the State.* Cambridge: Harvard University Press, 1989.

Maltz, Earl M. *Rethinking Constitutional Law: Originalism, Interventionism, and the Politics of Judicial Review.* Lawrence: University Press of Kansas, 1984.

Michael Martin. *The Legal Philosophy of H. L. A. Hart: A Critical Appraisal.* Philadelphia: Temple University Press, 1987.

Mill, John Stuart. *On Liberty.* New York: Penguin, 1976.

——. *The Subjection of Women.* Indianapolis: Hackett, 1988.

Miller, Arthur. *The Assault on Privacy.* Cambridge: Harvard University Press, 1971.

Minow, Martha. *Making All the Difference: Inclusion, Exclusion, and American Law.* Ithaca: Cornell University Press, 1990.

Mohr, Richard A. *Gays/Justice.* New York: Columbia University Press, 1988.

O'Brien, David. *Privacy, Law, and Public Policy.* New York: Praeger Special Studies, 1979.

———. *The Right to Privacy: Its Constitutional and Social Dimensions: A Comprehensive Bibliography.* Austin: Tarlton Law Library, University of Texas Law School, 1980.

Okin, Susan Moller. *Justice, Gender, and the Family.* New York: Basic Books, 1989.

Pateman, Carole. *The Disorder of Women: Democracy, Feminism, and Political Theory.* Stanford: Stanford University Press, 1989.

Pennock, J. Roland, and John W. Chapman, eds. *Privacy.* Nomos 13. New York: Atherton Press, 1971.

Posner, Richard. *The Economics of Justice.* Cambridge: Harvard University Press, 1981.

Prosser, William L. *Handbook of the Law of Torts.* 2d ed. St. Paul, Minn.: West, 1955.

Richards, David A. J. *Toleration and the Constitution: A Theory of Religious Freedom, Free Speech, and Constitutional Privacy.* New York: Oxford University Press, 1986.

Sandel, Michael. *Democracy's Discontent: America in Search of a Public Philosophy.* Cambridge: Harvard University Press, 1996.

Scheppele, Kim Lane. *Legal Secrets.* Chicago: University of Chicago Press, 1988.

Schoeman, Ferdinand. *Privacy and Social Freedom.* Cambridge: Cambridge University Press, 1992.

———, ed. *Philosophical Dimensions of Privacy: An Anthology.* Cambridge: Cambridge University Press, 1984.

Shapiro, Ian, ed. *Abortion: The Supreme Court Decisions.* Cambridge, Mass.: Hackett, 1995.

Smith, Patricia, ed. *Feminist Jurisprudence.* Oxford: Oxford University Press, 1993.

———, ed. *The Nature and Process of Law.* Oxford: Oxford University Press, 1993.

Tribe, Laurence H. *American Constitutional Law.* 2d ed. Mineola, N.Y.: Foundation Press, 1988.

Tribe, Laurence H., and Michael C. Dorf. *On Reading the Constitution.* Cambridge: Harvard University Press, 1991.

Turkington, Richard C., George B. Trubow, and Anita L. Allen, eds. *Privacy: Cases and Materials.* Houston, Tex.: John Marshall, 1992.

Westin, Alan. *Privacy and Freedom.* New York: Atheneum Press, 1967.

Wueste, Daniel, ed. *AIDS: Crisis in Professional Ethics.* Philadelphia: Temple University Press, 1994.

Index

Judith Wagner DeCew
is Associate Professor of Philosophy
at Clark University.